Summary

In an increasingly global economy, and with retirement starting for the Baby Boomer generation, Congress has indicated a strong interest in ensuring that today's young people have the educational attainment and employment experience needed to become highly skilled workers, contributing taxpayers, and successful participants in civic life. Challenges in the economy and among certain youth populations, however, have heightened concern among policymakers that some young people may not be prepared to fill these roles.

The employment levels for youth under age 25 have declined markedly in recent years, including in the wake of the 2007-2009 recession. Certain young people—including high school dropouts, current and former foster youth, and other at-risk populations—face challenges in completing school and entering the workforce. While the United States has experienced a dramatic increase in secondary school achievement in the past several decades, approximately 9% of youth ages 18 through 24 have not attained a high school diploma or its equivalent. In addition, millions of young people are out of school and not working.

Since the 1930s, federal job training and employment programs and policies have sought to connect vulnerable youth to work and school. Generally, these young people have been defined as being at-risk because they are economically disadvantaged and have a barrier to employment. During the Great Depression, the focus was on employing young men who were idle through public works and other projects. The employment programs from this era included an educational component to encourage youth to obtain their high school diplomas. Beginning in the 1960s, the federal government began funding programs for low-income youth that address their multiple needs through job training, educational services, and supportive services.

Today's primary federal youth employment and job training programs are authorized under the Workforce Investment Act of 1998 (WIA, P.L. 105-220), and are carried out by the Department of Labor's (DOL's) Employment and Training Administration (ETA). Although these programs are funded somewhat differently and have varying eligibility requirements, they generally have a common purpose—to provide youth with educational and employment opportunities and access to leadership development and community service activities. Many of the programs target the most vulnerable youth, including school dropouts, homeless youth, and youth offenders. Based on funding and the number of youth served, the WIA Youth Activities (Youth) formula program and Job Corps are the largest. The Youth formula program provides an array of job training and other services through what are known as local workforce investment boards (WIBs). Job Corps provides training in a number of trades at centers where youth reside.

Another program, YouthBuild, engages youth in educational services and job training that focus on the construction trades. Separately, WIA's pilot and demonstration authority has been used to carry out the Reintegration of Ex-Offenders program, which provides job training and other services to juvenile and adult offenders. Finally, the Youth Opportunity Grant (YOG) program, which was funded until FY2003, was targeted to youth who lived in select high-poverty communities.

This report accompanies two reports—CRS Report R40930, *Vulnerable Youth: Issues in the Reauthorization of the Workforce Investment Act*; and CRS Report R40830, *Vulnerable Youth: Federal Funding for Summer Job Training and Employment*.

Contents

Tables

Appendixes

Contacts

Introduction

In an increasingly competitive economy, and with retirement starting for the Baby Boomer generation, Congress has indicated a strong interest in ensuring that today's young people have the educational attainment and employment experience necessary to become highly skilled workers, contributing taxpayers, and successful participants in civic life. Challenges in the economy and among vulnerable youth populations, however, have heightened concern among policymakers that many young people may not be prepared to fill these roles.

The employment levels for youth under age 25 have declined markedly in recent years, including in the wake of the recession that extended from December 2007 through June 2009. Certain young people in particular—including those from low-income families, high school dropouts, foster youth, and other at-risk populations—face barriers to completing school and entering the workforce. Since the 1960s, federal job training programs and policies have sought to connect these youth to education and employment pathways. Contemporary federal youth employment programs with this same purpose are authorized under the Workforce Investment Act (WIA) of 1998 (P.L. 105-220). These programs provide a range of services and supports to youth. They include the Youth Activities (Youth) formula grant program; Job Corps; YouthBuild; the Reintegration of Ex-Offenders program, which includes a youth component; and the Youth Opportunity Grant (YOG) program. Some of the programs concentrate on specific job trades and/or serve targeted at-risk populations. Based on funding, Job Corps and the Youth program are the largest.

This report provides an overview of federal employment programs for vulnerable young people. It begins with a discussion of the current challenges in preparing all youth today for the workforce. The report then provides a chronology of job training and employment programs for at-risk youth that began in the 1930s and were expanded or modified from the 1960s through the 1990s. It goes on to discuss the five youth programs authorized under WIA, and draws comparisons between these programs. Following this section is a detailed discussion of each of the programs. This report accompanies two CRS reports—CRS Report R40930, *Vulnerable Youth: Issues in the Reauthorization of the Workforce Investment Act*; and CRS Report R40830, *Vulnerable Youth: Federal Funding for Summer Job Training and Employment*.

Context

The recent economic recession that ended in June 2009 focused attention on the role of the federal and state governments in supporting workers who have been laid off or are at risk of being laid off. During economic downturns, youth are particularly vulnerable to job loss. From 2000 through 2011, the rate of employment[1] among teens steadily declined.[2] Over the summer, when teens are most likely to have jobs, the rate of employment decreased most steeply. In July 2000,

---

[1] The employment rate, or the *employment to population ratio (E/P ratio)*, is the proportion of individuals in the population as a whole who are employed.

[2] U.S. Department of Labor, Bureau of Labor Statistics, *The Employment Situation*, http://www.bls.gov/schedule/ archives/empsit_nr htm; and Andrew Sum, Iswhar Khatiwada, and Sheila Palma, *The Continued Collapse of the Nation's Teen Summer Job Market: Who Worked in the Summer of 2011?*, Center for Labor Market Studies, Northeastern University, September 2011 (Hereinafter, Sum, McLaughlin, and Palma, *The Continued Collapse of the Nation's Teen Summer Job Market: Who Worked in the Summer of 2011?),*

slightly less than half (44.1%) of all teens were employed, compared to 25.4% in July 2011.[3] The July 2011 employment rate was the lowest it had been during the post-World War II period. The declining rate of teen employment overall appears to be attributable to rising levels of joblessness and not to a declining interest in employment among teens.[4] According to the research literature, possible consequences of reduced work among teens are reduced employment earnings, labor productivity in the future, and output in the economy. Similarly, the employment rates of young adults ages 20 through 24 have declined steadily.[5] In 2010, the average employment rate for 20- through 24-year-olds was 60.8%, which represents about a 16% decrease from 2000.[6] The employment-to-population ratio for young adults was the second lowest (after 2010) it has been in approximately 60 years.

Rates of employment among young people vary based on income. An analysis by the Center for Labor Market Studies shows the employment rate of teens ages 16 through 19 increases as household incomes increase.[7] In 2011, about one out of every five teens in households with earnings below $20,000 worked, compared to about one-third of teens with household incomes of $40,000 to $60,000 and $60,000 to $75,000, and 37.2% of teens in households with incomes of $75,000 to $100,000.

Even in periods of relative economic stability, some youth do not complete school and/or make the transition to the workforce. While the majority of young people graduate from (public) high school by age 18 or shortly thereafter,[8] about 9% of youth ages 16 through 24 have dropped out and have not earned a high school diploma or its equivalent.[9] This figure is higher among black and Hispanic youth.[10] Further, recent estimates of youth who are not working or in school (i.e., "disconnected") for at least a year are approximately 2.6 million.[11] Certain youth face barriers to remaining in school or securing employment, including poverty, their parents' level of education,

---

[3] U.S. Department of Labor, Bureau of Labor Statistics, *Labor Force Statistics from the Current Population Survey*, http://data.bls.gov/pdq/querytool.jsp?survey=ln. (Hereinafter U.S. Department of Labor, Bureau of Labor Statistics, *Labor Force Statistics from the Current Population Survey*.)

[4] Ibid.

[5] Andrew Sum, Joseph McLaughlin, and Sheila Palma, *The Collapse of the Nation's Male Teen and Young Adult Labor Market, 2000-2009: The Lost Generation of Young Male Workers*, Center for Labor Market Studies, Northeastern University, prepared for C.S. Mott Foundation, July 2009, http://www.nyec.org/content/documents/ThecollapseoftheNation'sMaleTeenandYoungAdult.pdf.

[6] U.S. Department of Labor, Bureau of Labor Statistics, *Labor Force Statistics from the Current Population Survey*.

[7] Sum, McLaughlin, and Palma, *The Continued Collapse of the Nation's Teen Summer Job Market: Who Worked in the Summer of 2011*. See also, Andrew Sum and Ishwar Khatiwada with Sheila Palma, *Dire Straits in the Nation's Teen Labor Market: The Outlook for the Summer 2010 Teen Job Market and the Case for a Comprehensive Youth Jobs Creation Strategy*, Northeastern University, Center for Labor Market Studies, Prepared for C.S. Mott Foundation, April 2010, pp. 7-8, http://www.seakingwdc.org/pdf/other-reports/AndySumYouthEmpReport_4-10.pdf.

[8] The average freshman graduation rate (AFGR) is an estimate of the percentage of an entering public school freshman class graduating in four years. For the most recent school years, the AFGR has been about 75%. Of the 25% of youth who do not graduate in four years, some continue in school because they have a learning disability or for other reasons; however, many of these youth drop out, with some returning to school at a later time while they are working or are idle. U.S. Department of Education, National Center for Education Statistics, *The Condition of Education 2011*, Table A-18-1, *Averaged Freshman Graduation Rate for Public High School Students and Number of Graduates, by State: School years 2000–01 through 2008-2009*, May 2011, http://nces.ed.gov/pubs2011/2011033.pdf.

[9] Ibid, Table A-20-1, *Status Dropout Rates of 16- Through 24-year-olds in the Civilian, Noninstitutionalized Population, by Race/ethnicity: October Current Population Survey (CPS) 1980–2009*.

[10] Ibid.

[11] CRS Report R40535, *Disconnected Youth: A Look at 16- to 24-Year Olds Who Are Not Working or In School*, by Adrienne L. Fernandes-Alcantara and Thomas Gabe.

and whether the youth are pregnant or parenting, among other factors. For example, youth ages 16 through 24 who are parenting are far more likely to be disconnected than their counterparts who are not.[12] Youth in or aging out of foster care, runaway and homeless youth, and youth offenders, among other groups of youth, are particularly vulnerable to not completing high school, going on to college, or securing employment.[13] For example, in a study of youth who had been in foster care and were, on average, about age 25, most had obtained a high school diploma or passed the general education development (GED) test at about the same rate as young people ages 18 to 29 in the general population. However, they were much less likely to have a bachelor's degree—1.8% versus 22.5% of all young people.[14] Further, the employment rate for these foster care alumni was 80%, while the employment rate for their counterparts in the general population was 95%.

As they leave high school, either through graduation or by dropping out, young people can pursue various options. Youth with a high school diploma may attend a two- or four-year college, enlist in the armed services, or secure part-time or full-time employment (sometimes paired with attending school). Youth without a high school diploma can do some of these same things, but their opportunities are more limited. They cannot enroll in a four-year college or, in most cases, enlist in the military. These youth will likely have difficulty supporting themselves if they do work.

In fact, individuals who drop out are less likely to secure employment and are likely to have less earning power. As the level of education rises, the unemployment rate decreases and median weekly earnings increase for those who work.[15] In 2011, among workers with less than a high school degree, the unemployment rate was 14.1% and earnings averaged $451 per week. This is compared to an unemployment rate of 9.4% and $638 in weekly earnings for workers with a high school degree. Workers with a bachelor's degree had an unemployment rate of 4.9% and median weekly earnings of $1,053. With the shift to a knowledge-based economy, most new jobs will require some college education or better.[16] According to the Bureau of Labor Statistics, by 2018 nearly two-thirds of all job openings will require at least a bachelor's degree, compared to about one-third of all new jobs in 2008.[17]

The costs of dropping out extend beyond the individual's foregone job opportunities and lower wages.[18] According to the research literature, costs can be incurred by society overall. These costs

---

[12] Ibid.

[13] For further information about the challenges certain groups of youth face while making the transition to adulthood, see CRS Report RL33975, *Vulnerable Youth: Background and Policies*, by Adrienne L. Fernandes-Alcantara.

[14] Peter J. Pecora et al., *Improving Foster Family Care: Findings from the Northwest Foster Care Alumni Study*, Casey Family Programs, 2005, http://www.casey.org/Resources/Publications/ImprovingFamilyFosterCare.htm.

[15] U.S. Department of Labor, Bureau of Labor Statistics, Current Population Survey; *Education Pays*, March 23, 2012, http://www.bls.gov/emp/ep_chart_001 htm.

[16] T. Alan Lacey and Benjamin Wright, "Occupational Employment Projections to 2018," *Monthly Labor Review*, vol. 132, no. 11 (November 2009), pp. 88, 90, http://www.bls.gov/opub/mlr/2009/11/art5full.pdf (Hereinafter, Lacey and Wright, "Occupational Employment Projections to 2018."). See also, Anthony P. Carnevale, Nicole Smith, and Jeff Strohl, *Help Wanted: Projections of Jobs and Education Requirements through 2018*, Georgetown University, Center on Education and the Workforce, June 2010, http://cew.georgetown.edu/JOBS2018/.

[17] Lacey and Wright, "Occupational Employment Projections to 2018."

[18] Northeastern University, Center for Labor Market Studies, The Consequences of Dropping Out of High School: Joblessness and Jailing of High School Dropouts and the High Cost for Taxpayers, May 5, 2009, http://iris.lib.neu.edu/cgi/viewcontent.cgi?article=1020&context=clms_pub; Paul E. Barton, One Third of a Nation: Rising Dropout Rates and Declining Opportunities, Educational Testing Services, February 2009, http://www.ets.org/Media/ (continued...)

---

include possible lost payroll tax revenue and increased transfers for welfare payments, imprisonment, and programs to re-enroll dropouts in school.

Federal youth employment and job training programs have long targeted services to young people who leave school before graduating or are in school and may be vulnerable to dropping out. The purpose of these programs, as they currently exist, is to provide job training, employment, educational services, and social services that can help youth become economically self-sufficient and achieve their career and academic goals. These contemporary programs also emphasize leadership development and community service. Note that while youth employment and job training programs are also enhanced with state workforce and other dollars, the extent to which this support is provided is unclear.

History of Federal Youth Employment and Job Training Programs[19]

For more than 70 years, the federal government has played a role in helping young people secure employment and achieve academic success. Generally, these young people have been defined as being vulnerable in some way—either because they are economically disadvantaged and/or have a barrier to securing employment or completing their education. During the Great Depression, the focus was on employing idle young men in public works and other projects. The employment programs from this era included an educational component to encourage youth to obtain their high school diplomas. Beginning in the 1960s, the federal government started funding programs for low-income youth, such as Job Corps, that address their multiple needs, including job training, educational services, housing, and supportive services. During the 1970s and 1980s, Job Corps was expanded and the federal government funded additional programs for both in-school and out-of-school youth. Funding was also appropriated to test the efficacy of some of these programs. The Workforce Investment Act of 1998 extended earlier programs and created new ones, with the intention of providing more seamless job training and education services for youth year-round. Generally, these programs are targeted to teenagers and young adults, usually not beyond age 24, who are at risk of dropping out or have already done so.

Depression Era

Prior to the 1930s, the federal government's involvement in youth employment was primarily limited to regulating child labor.[20] The Great Depression served as a catalyst for the creation of federal programs to employ and educate young people who were out of work or at risk of dropping out of school due to financial difficulties. The Civilian Conservation Corps (CCC)

(...continued)

Education_Topics/pdf/onethird.pdf. Clive R. Belfield, Henry M. Levin, and Rachel Rosen, The Economic Value of Opportunity Youth, prepared for the Corporation for National and Community Service and the White House Council for Economic Solutions, January 2012, http://www.serve.gov/new-images/council/pdf/ econ_value_opportunity_youth.pdf.

[19] Unless otherwise noted, this section draws heavily on an archived report by the Congressional Research Service, *Youth Employment: A Summary History of Major Federal Programs*, 1933-1976. Available upon request.

[20] John H. Bremner, Tamara K. Hareven, and Robert M. Mennel, eds., *Children & Youth in America*, Vol. II: 1866-1932, Parts 1-6 (Cambridge, MA: Harvard University Press, 1971), pp. 687-749.

began in 1933 as an employment program for unemployed males ages 18 to 25 (and veterans, Indians, and residents of territories of any age) to participate in projects planned by the Departments of the Interior and Agriculture. These projects focused on creating and improving infrastructure, transportation, and recreational services, among other categories. The young men lived in camps and were provided with an allowance, food, and medical care. The CCC also included an educational component, which taught nearly 35,000 participants to read and write and assisted a smaller number with attaining their high school and college degrees. Until the program ended in 1945, it served nearly 3 million men, of whom approximately 10% were veterans.

Other Depression era programs—the Student Aid program, Works Project program, and Guidance and Placement program—were administered by the National Youth Administration, which was created as part of the now-defunct Works Progress Administration by an executive order in 1935. The programs provided funds for part-time employment of needy high school, college, and graduate students to assist them in completing school, as well as funds for part-time employment for unemployed out-of-school youth. These young people, all of whom were ages 16 through 25, were employed in a number of broad areas, including construction, clerical work, and research. These programs served hundreds of thousands of youth before they were discontinued in the early 1940s.

War on Poverty Programs

The 1960s marked a period of federal efforts to assist poor and disadvantaged children, adolescents, and their families through job training and other programs. In response to concerns about high unemployment, the Manpower Development and Training Act of 1962 (P.L. 87-415) and subsequent amendments to it authorized funding for employment training. Specifically, amendments to the act in 1963 (P.L. 88-214) encouraged the Department of Labor to provide assistance to youth so that they might be able to successfully enter the labor force, and expanded the share of job training funds that could be used to train youth under age 22 from 5% to 25%. Further, federal funding was first authorized through the 1963 amendments to provide employment opportunities to youth from low-income families.

President Lyndon B. Johnson's subsequent War on Poverty established new youth-targeted programs in job training and educational assistance under an initiative known as the Neighborhood Youth Corps (NYC). The NYC was comprised of work training programs, the Work Study program, and Job Corps. The work training programs provided work experience, job training, and supportive services to low-income unemployed youth ages 16 through 21 who were in school or out of school, including dropouts. The Work Study program was modeled on the Depression-era Student Aid program and provided money to high school and college students from low-income families who needed earnings to stay in school. The program continues today for college students. Job Corps, which also continues today, was established under the Economic Opportunity Act of 1964 (P.L. 88-452) to provide educational and job training opportunities to disadvantaged youth at residential and non-residential centers. (See "Job Corps," below, for further information.)

Expanding Youth Programs

The 1973 Comprehensive Employment and Training Act (CETA, P.L. 93-203) was the first of four laws enacted during the 1970s and 1980s that focused greater federal attention on youth employment and training. The second law, the Youth Employment and Demonstrations Project

Act (YEDPA, P.L. 95-93) was enacted in 1977 and established a variety of employment, training, and demonstration programs for youth. The 1982 Job Training Partnership Act (JTPA, P.L. 97-300) repealed CETA. JTPA was subsequently repealed by WIA. Separately, the School-to-Work Opportunities Act of 1994 (STWOA, P.L. 103-239) supported the development of programs that encouraged students to pursue learning opportunities and experiences that incorporated occupational skills. Activities authorized under these acts were administered by DOL. STWOA was additionally carried out by the Department of Education (ED).

CETA and YEDPA

As amended through 1978, CETA authorized a range of employment and training programs for adults and youth. Job Corps and the Summer Program for Economically Disadvantaged Youth (SPEDY) were the primary youth programs authorized under CETA. SPEDY provided funding to employers to hire low-income youth ages 14 through 21 during the summer months. Youth served as assistants in hospitals, libraries, community service organizations, and schools, among other settings.

The Youth Employment and Demonstrations Project Act (YEDPA), signed into law in 1977, amended CETA.[21] YEDPA increased authorization of appropriations for Job Corps and SPEDY and authorized three additional programs targeted to "economically disadvantaged" (defined under the act) youth ages 14 through 21: Youth Employment and Training Programs (YETP), Youth Community Conservation and Improvement Projects (YCCIP), and Youth Incentive Entitlement Pilot Projects (YIEPP).[22] YEDPA was passed in response to high levels of unemployment among youth relative to adults, even during periods of economic expansion, and growing gaps in youth unemployment among whites and blacks, males and females, and in-school and out-of-school youth. The programs were carried out during the Carter Administration, from 1977 through 1981. Over this period, YEDPA served 6.1 million youth.

YETP and YCCIP were intended to meet the immediate employment needs of youth, and funding for the programs was allocated primarily on a formula basis. YETP activities include work experience, pre-employment skills, and an emphasis on the transition from school to work. YCCIP was intended to assist unemployed, out-of-school youth obtain a high school degree, conditional on satisfactory performance in work and school. Further, it was aimed at improving coordination between the job training and educational systems as a means of addressing the dropout problem.[23] Finally, YIEPP funded evaluations to test the efficacy of demonstration

---

[21] Much of this section on YEDPA was drawn from Charles L. Betsey, Robinson G. Hollister, and Mary R. Papageorgiou, eds., *Youth Employment and Training Programs: The YEDPA Years*, National Research Council, Washington, DC, 1985, http://www.eric.ed.gov/ERICWebPortal/custom/portlets/recordDetails/detailmini.jsp?_nfpb= true&_&ERICExtSearch_SearchValue_0=ED265245&ERICExtSearch_SearchType_0=no&accno=ED265245. (Hereinafter, Betsey, Hollister, and Papageorgiou, *Youth Employment and Training Programs*.)

[22] A fourth, the Young Adult Conservation Corps (YACC), was operated by the Department of Agriculture and Department of the Interior, in cooperation with DOL, and targeted unemployed youth ages 16 to 23 who were not necessarily disadvantaged. This program operated year-round and was separate from a similarly named program, the Youth Conservation Corps (YCC). YCC was permanently authorized by the Youth Conservation Corps Act of 1970 (P.L. 91-378) and continues to operate.

[23] Other parts of YEDPA required close coordination with the school system. According to an assessment of the act's implementation, the schools maintained their focus on in-school youth and provided essentially the same set of educational services as usual. The lack of influence of YEDPA on schools may be largely attributed to the schools' resistance to allocating services according to income and the schools' perception that their mission was exclusively to educate students. Betsey, Hollister, and Papageorgiou, *Youth Employment and Training Programs*, pp. 84-87.

---

programs; the other two programs included funding for demonstration programs. During the YEDPA years, more than 60 major demonstrations were funded in about 300 sites, operated by DOL in cooperation with six other federal agencies and private nonprofit intermediaries.

JTPA[24]

CETA was repealed in 1982 by the Job Training Partnership Act. JTPA was distinct from its predecessor because it emphasized that states and localities, rather than the federal government, had the primary responsibility for administering job training and employment programs. Funding was appropriated under JTPA through FY1999. JTPA programs focused on the training needs of "economically disadvantaged" (defined under the act) youth and adults facing significant barriers to employment. These programs were frequently referred to as "second chance" programs because most of them were intended to train individuals who had not sufficiently benefitted from traditional secondary and post-secondary education. They included the Summer Youth Employment and Training program, the Youth Training Program, and Job Corps (discussed in the next section).

The Summer Youth Employment and Training program provided employment and training activities during the summer months for low-income youth ages 14 through 21 to strengthen basic educational skills, encourage school completion, provide work exposure, and enhance citizenship skills. In the summer of 1997, an estimated 500,000 youth participated. The Youth Training Program was established by the Job Training Reform Amendments of 1992 (P.L. 102-367), which amended JTPA to address concerns that school dropouts were not being reached by the then-existing combined program for disadvantaged adults and youth, and that the program primarily served youth who were the easiest to place in jobs and required the fewest services.[25] The program was year-round and provided direct services, such as on-the-job training, tutoring and study skills training, and school-to-work transition services. It also provided training-related and supportive services, including job search assistance, drug and alcohol abuse counseling, and cash incentives based on attendance and performance in a program. Economically disadvantaged in-school and out-of-school youth ages 16 through 21 were eligible, but 50% of participants in service delivery areas (SDAs), comprised of the state or one or more units of local government, had to be out of school. Further, at least 65% of youth had to be hard to serve, meaning they were school dropouts (if out of school), pregnant or parenting, or offenders, among other qualifications. In program year 1997, an estimated 107,000 youth participated. As discussed below, JTPA was repealed by WIA, the current law that authorizes youth job training and employment programs.

STWOA

The School to Work Opportunity Act of 1994 authorized the School-to-Work (STW) program administered jointly by DOL and the Department of Education through the National School-to-Work Office. The program was funded from FY1994 through FY2000.[26] The law supported the

---

[24] Unless otherwise noted, this section was drawn heavily from an archived report by the Congressional Research Service, *The Job Training Partnership Act: A Compendium of Programs*. Available upon request.

[25] Archived report by the Congressional Research Service, *Job Training Partnership Act: Legislation and Budget Issues*. Available upon request.

[26] Archived report by the Congressional Research Service, *The School-to-Work Opportunities Act*. Available upon request.

development of programs with three main elements: work-based learning to provide participating students with work experience and on-the-job training; school-based learning, involving upgrading and integrating the occupational skills participating students learn in school and the workplace; and program coordination to aid the planning, implementation, and operation of the program. STWOA grants were competitively awarded to states, local partnerships, programs for Indian youth, and U.S. territories to implement school-to-work systems. In addition, STWOA authorized national activities, such as research and demonstrations. Some school-to-work programs that received seed money from the federal program continue to operate today.

WIA

The Workforce Investment Act of 1998 replaced JTPA. WIA includes titles that authorize programs for job training and related services (Title I), adult education and literacy (Title II), employment services (Title III), and vocational rehabilitation (Title IV). Title I of WIA authorizes job training programs for youth, adults, and dislocated workers.[27] As described by DOL in a 2000 Training and Employment Guidance Letter (TEGL) to state and local workforce development boards, WIA places "new emphasis on serving youth within a comprehensive statewide workforce development system." The programs for youth are discussed in further detail below.

Overview of Youth Programs Authorized Under Title I of the Workforce Investment Act

Job training and employment services for youth under WIA include

- *Youth Activities*, a formula grant program for states that includes employment and other services that are provided year-round;

- *Job Corps*, a program that provides job training and related services primarily at residential centers maintained by contractor organizations;

- *YouthBuild*, a competitive grant program that emphasizes job training and education in construction;

- *Reintegration of Ex-Offenders*, a demonstration program for juvenile and adult offenders that provides job training and other services and is authorized under WIA's pilot and demonstration authority; and

- *Youth Opportunity Grants* program, a multi-site demonstration program funded through FY2003 that created centers in low-income communities where youth could receive employment and other services.

WIA's authorization of appropriations expired at the end of FY2003. However, Congress continues to appropriate funds, including those for youth job training programs—except for the Youth Opportunity Grants program, which has not been funded since FY2003. All of the

---

[27] For further information about the Adult and Dislocated Worker programs, see CRS Report RL33687, *The Workforce Investment Act (WIA): Program-by-Program Overview and Funding of Title I Training Programs*, by David H. Bradley.

programs are carried out by DOL's Employment and Training Administration (ETA).[28] As mentioned above, Job Corps was enacted as part of the Economic Opportunity Act of 1964 (P.L. 88-452), and was later incorporated into CETA and JTPA. YouthBuild was originally authorized under the Cranston-Gonzalez National Affordable Housing Act of 1992 (P.L. 102-550). The program was administered by the Department of Housing and Urban Development (HUD) until it was transferred to DOL in 2007 under the YouthBuild Transfer Act (P.L. 109-281) and incorporated into WIA.

All of the programs offer employment, job training, and educational services. For example, local areas must provide 10 specific elements, including mentoring and follow-up, to youth who receive services under the Youth Activities formula grant program. YouthBuild program participants engage in employment and other activities primarily related to housing and other types of construction work. Job Corps is the only one of the programs that provides residential services; youth can live onsite and receive health care services, child care, and other supports. As with Job Corps, the YOG program established centers, albeit non-residential, where youth could receive employment and other services. Further, the programs generally serve vulnerable youth, but some have more targeted eligibility criteria. Participants in the Youth Activities formula grant program, YouthBuild, and Job Corps must be low-income and have specific employment barriers. The youth component of the Reintegration of Ex-Offenders serves youth who have become involved in the juvenile justice or criminal justice system or youth at risk of becoming involved. When the YOG program was in operation, youth automatically qualified for the program if they lived in low-income communities. Finally, the programs are funded somewhat differently. DOL allocates funding for Youth Activities to states based on a formula, while Job Corps enters into agreements with nonprofit and for-profit organizations and other federal agencies. The other programs competitively award grants to nonprofit and other organizations and local communities.

Coordination

Together, the WIA Youth program and other WIA programs collectively make up a job training and workforce system for youth. In some cases, WIA includes provisions that encourage or require the programs to coordinate with one another. In submitting their state workforce investment plans to DOL, states must specify how they will coordinate Youth Activities programming with services provided by Job Corps centers in places where they exist. In addition, youth councils, comprised of stakeholders with an interest in the employment and other needs of youth, must include representatives from Job Corps, where applicable. Further, Youth Activities, Job Corps, and YouthBuild are required partners at one-stop centers. One-stop centers include approximately 20 federal programs that coordinate employment and other services in a community for all youth and adults.

The White House Task Force for Disadvantaged Youth, convened in 2002 under President George W. Bush, sought to improve coordination of youth programs across the federal government and use federal resources to assist the neediest youth, including those who would be eligible for programs under Title I of WIA. In response, ETA established the Shared Youth Vision, which is intended to connect the most at-risk youth to work and school.[29] As part of these efforts, DOL has

---

[28] The Office of Job Corps is being transferred from the Office of the Secretary to ETA pursuant to the Consolidated Appropriations Act, 2010 (P.L. 111-117).

[29] U.S. Department of Labor, Employment and Training Administration, TEGL No. 3-04 ("The Employment and Training Administration's (ETA's) new strategic vision to serve out-of-school and at-risk youth under the Workforce (continued...)

partnered with other federal agencies, including the U.S. Departments of Education, Health and Human Services, and Justice to improve communication and collaboration across programs that target at-risk youth groups under an initiative called the "Shared Youth Vision."[30] Together, the agencies convened an Interagency Work Group and conducted regional forums to develop and coordinate policies and research on the vulnerable youth population. The purpose of these forums was to create and implement plans to improve communication and collaboration between local organizations that serve at-risk youth. DOL competitively awarded grants totaling $1.6 million to 16 states to assist them in developing strategic plans to link their systems that serve youth.

Funding

Funding authorization for the youth programs under WIA expired in FY2003.[31] Although funding authorization has expired, Congress has continued to appropriate funds for most programs authorized under the law. **Table 1** includes the funds appropriated for FY2000 through FY2012 and funds proposed for FY2013. Congress appropriated $2.6 billion to $2.9 billion in most years over this period.[32] **Table A-1** in **Appendix A** presents Youth Activities funding allocated to the states and outlying areas for PY2008 through PY2012 (the most recent data available), including under the American Reinvestment and Recovery Act (ARRA, P.L. 111-5), the law that provided additional funding to create and preserve jobs, among other purposes.

Of programs that continue to be funded,[33] Job Corps has received the largest appropriation each year, followed by the Youth Activities formula grant program, YouthBuild, and the youth component of the Reintegration of Ex-Offenders (although in two years, YouthBuild received less funding than the Reintegration of Ex-Offenders' youth component).[34] Funding for Job Corps has increased over this period, from $1.4 billion in FY2000 to $1.7 billion in FY2012. In contrast, funding for Youth Activities has decreased, from $1.0 billion in FY2000 to $824.4 million in FY2012. Funding has fluctuated for the other two major programs, YouthBuild and the youth component of the Reintegration of Ex-Offenders Program. Funding for YouthBuild in FY2010 was $102.5 million, the highest level to date, but decreased to $79.8 million in FY2011 and further to $79.7 million in FY2012. In FY2009, the youth component of the Reintegration of Ex-Offenders program was $88.5 million, the highest level to date, but decreased to $50 million in FY2011.

(...continued)

Investment Act (WIA)"), July 16, 2004.

[30] U.S. Department of Labor, Employment and Training Administration, "Shared Youth Vision, Mission and Objectives," http://www.doleta.gov/ryf/whitehousereport/vmo.cfm.

[31] Congress may sometimes choose to appropriate funds even after the expiration of the funding authorization.

[32] The total funding for FY2012 will be available once DOL determines the level of funding for the youth component of the Reintegration of Ex-Offenders program.

[33] The Youth Opportunity Grants program was funded from FY1999 through FY2003, and was operational through FY2005. The program received between $225,100 and $250,000 in each of FY2000 through FY2002 and $44,211 in FY2003.

[34] FY2012 funding data was included in the conference report (H.Rept. 112-331) for the Consolidated Appropriations Act, FY2012 (P.L. 112-74). This law was the final in a series of continuing resolutions to provide funding for the Department of Labor and select other departments. The funding data presented in the conference report does not include the across-the-board rescission of 0.189%. The figures presented in this report are based on estimates made by the Congressional Research Service that incorporate this rescission.

Table 1. Funding for DOL Youth Job Training and Employment Programs, Appropriations for FY2000-FY2012 and Proposed Funding for FY2013

(dollars in thousands)

Fiscal Year	Youth Activities	Job Corps	YouthBuild[a]	Youth Offenders (Reintegration of Ex-Offenders)[b]	Total Funding, All Programs
FY2000	$1,000,965	$1,357,776	$43,000	$13,907	$2,415,648
FY2001	1,127,965	1,399,148	60,000	55,000	2,642,113
FY2002	1,127,965	1,458,732	65,000	55,000	2,706,697
FY2003	994,459	1,509,094	59,610	54,643	2,617,806
FY2004	995,059	1,541,151	65,000	49,705	2,650,915
FY2005	986,288	1,551,861	62,000	69,440	2,669,589
FY2006	940,500	1,564,180	62,000	49,104	2,615,784
FY2007	940,500	1,566,178	49,500	49,104	2,605,282
FY2008	924,069	1,610,506	58,952	55,000	2,648,527
FY2009	924,069	1,683,938	70,000	88,500	2,766,507
ARRA	1,200,000	250,000	50,000	0	1,500,000
FY2010	924,069	1,708,205	102,500	73,493	2,808,267
FY2011[c]	825,914	1,706,171[d]	79,840	50,000[e]	2,661,925
FY2012[f]	824,353	1,702,947	79,689	—[f]	—[g]
FY2013	824,353	1,650,004	79,689	—[h]	—[h]

Source: Compiled by the Congressional Research Service (CRS) from Department of Labor (DOL) budget justifications; Department of Housing and Urban Development (HUD) budget justifications; DOL Employment and Training Administration budget information at http://www.doleta.gov/budget; correspondence with DOL, July 2010 and January 2011; DOL, *All Purpose Table FY2011 Full-Year Continuing Resolution*, http://www.dol.gov/dol/budget/2012/PDF/2011OperatingPlanTable.pdf; U.S. Congress, Conference Report to Accompany H.R. 2055, *Military Construction and Veterans Affairs and Related Agencies Appropriations Act, 2012* Division F, 112th Cong., 1st sess., December 15, 2011, H.Rept. 112-331; and U.S. Department of Labor, *FY2013 Congressional Budget Justification, Employment and Training Administration, Training and Employment Services and Job Corps*, http://www.dol.gov/dol/budget/.

a. YouthBuild was transferred from HUD to DOL under the YouthBuild Transfer Act (P.L. 109-281).

b. Prior to FY2008, the Reintegration of Youthful Offenders program was a stand-alone program. It is now part of the Reintegration of Ex-Offenders program, which includes funding for juvenile and adult activities. Funding for the program is authorized under Section 171 (Demonstration and pilot projects) of WIA and Section 112 (Responsible reintegration of offenders) of the recently enacted Second Chance Act (P.L. 110-199). Section 112 authorizes DOL to make grants to nonprofit organizations for the purpose of providing mentoring, job training and job placement services, and other comprehensive transitional services to assist eligible offenders ages 18 and older in obtaining and retaining employment.

c. The Department of Defense and Full-Year Continuing Appropriations Act, 2011 (P.L. 112-10) includes a 0.2% across-the-board rescission.

d. Job Corps includes three accounts—administration, operations, and construction. The FY2011 appropriations law is based on funding for FY2010, and includes an across-the-board rescission of 0.2% for all programs and an additional rescission of $75 million. The 0.2% across-the-board rescission applies only to current year, and not advance, appropriations. Advance appropriations are those funds enacted in one fiscal year but not available for obligation until a subsequent fiscal year or years. Two of Job Corps' three accounts, operations and construction, include advance funds. Therefore, the across-the-board reduction only applies to current year funding (or $983.0 million for operations and $5.0 million for construction). According to the Department of Labor, $75 million was subtracted from existing balances, and therefore the FY2011 funding is not affected by this decrease. Congressional Research Service correspondence with the U.S. Department of Labor, Employment and Training Administration, May 2010.

e.   According to DOL, $50 million will be used for the youth component. In addition to the $50 million, one of the grants (funded at $12 million) will allow grantees to serve either youth or adult ex-offenders. Congressional Research Service correspondence with the U.S. Department of Labor, Employment and Training Administration, May 2012.

f.   FY2012 funding information was included in the conference report (H.Rept. 112-331) for the Consolidated Appropriations Act, FY2012 (P.L. 112-74). This law was the final in a series of continuing resolutions to provide funding for the Department of Labor and select other departments. The figures presented in the conference report do not include the across-the-board rescission of 0.189%. The figures presented in this incorporate this rescission.

g.   The FY2012 appropriations law provides funding of $85.2 million for the Reintegration of Ex-Offenders program; however, the law does not specify the amount of funding for the youth component. Final funding data are forthcoming from DOL.

h.   The FY2013 request for appropriations of $85.2 million does not specify the amount of funding for the youth component of the Reintegration of Ex-Offenders program.

FY2013 Request

For FY2013, the Administration has prioritized the following activities for each of the youth programs:

- Youth Activities: According to DOL, the department plans to (1) increase the share of youth who have credentials needed for careers, especially in high-growth sectors such as health care; (2) facilitate connections between youth seeking jobs and businesses seeking workers, particularly businesses in the private sector; and (3) assist local programs in developing collaborative partnerships with the Department of Health and Human Services (which administers the Temporary Assistance for Needy Families (TANF) program), the Departments of the Interior and Agriculture (which provide work experiences for youth on public lands), and the Department of Education (to improve literacy for out-of-school youth), among other departments. In addition, DOL would set aside $10 million in the Workforce Innovation fund (see next section of the report) to fund projects that focus on improving services for disconnected youth, or those who are not working or in school. These funds would address (1) limited knowledge of what program models are most effective in helping disconnected youth achieve positive outcomes; (2) a perceived lack of attention on this population at the state, local, and federal levels, and lack of coordination in addressing their needs; and (3) the need for more comprehensive approaches to meet the needs of this population.

- Job Corps: Job Corps has plans to initiate an agenda for improving its outcomes and strengthening accountability. DOL proposes closing "a small number of chronically low-performing" centers. The budget request does not specify criteria that would be used to identify such centers but it notes that these criteria will be shared with the public in advance. DOL further proposes to shift its focus toward strategies that were proven cost effective in evaluations of the Job Corps program, such as serving more youth ages 20 through 24.[35]

- YouthBuild: The agency intends to continue efforts in building the quality of existing YouthBuild programs through technical assistance efforts. DOL plans to continue a pilot with HHS's Substance Abuse and Mental Health Services Administration (SAMHSA) for identifying substance use and risk of substance use among participants. According to DOL, the program will focus on creating employment and apprenticeship opportunities for youth through partnerships with DOL's Office of Federal Contract Compliance Programs and the National Office of Apprenticeship.

- Reintegration of Ex-Offenders: DOL intends to fund competitive grants to national and regional intermediaries for activities that prepare young ex-offenders and school dropouts for employment. In addition, DOL plans to partner with the Department of Justice (DOJ) to support innovative models to reduce youth involvement in the juvenile justice system and/or recidivism and improve education and employment outcomes. The budget request goes on to explain that DOL will continue its partnership with DOJ's Coordinating Council on Juvenile Justice and Delinquency Prevention and other federal agencies to leverage additional federal resources for this population.

FY2012 and FY2011 Funding—Workforce Innovation Fund

In addition to the funds appropriated to the youth programs authorized under WIA, Congress provided additional funding for the Workforce Innovation Fund, a grant program to supplement funding for the Youth Activities program (along with the Adult and Dislocated Worker programs). These funds are intended to support projects that demonstrate innovative strategies or replicate evidence-based strategies that strengthen the workforce investment system and ultimately benefit the education and employment of participants.

In December 2011, DOL issued a solicitation announcing the availability of funding for the Workforce Innovation Fund. The solicitation provides examples of projects targeted to vulnerable youth. For instance, the solicitation states that projects can connect "the multiple systems that serve disconnected youth" to support summer employment and educational work experiences or improve coordination among existing programs, such as Job Corps and YouthBuild.[36]

ARRA Funding

ARRA provided additional funding to states and localities for the youth programs. As stated in the law, its purposes were to stimulate economic activity in selected industrial sectors to save existing jobs and create new jobs, reduce taxes, invest in future technologies, and fund infrastructure

---

[35] Peter Z. Schochet, John Burghardt, and Sheena McConnell, National Job Corps Study and Longer-Term Follow-Up Study: Impact and Benefit-Cost Findings Using Survey and Summary Earnings Records Data, August 2006, http://wdr.doleta.gov/research/FullText_Documents/ National%20Job%20Corps%20Study%20and%20Longer%20Term%20Follow-Up%20Study%20- %20Final%20Report.pdf.

[36] U.S. Department of Labor, Employment and Training Administration, "Notice of Availability of Funds and Solicitation for Grant Applications for Workforce Innovation Fund Grants," December 22, 2011.

---

improvements. The law appropriated $1.2 billion for grants for Youth Activities, $250 million for Job Corps, and $50 million for YouthBuild. In the accompanying conference report to ARRA, Congress specified that funds for the Youth Activities program should be used for summer youth employment and to expand year-round employment opportunities for youth up to age 24 (from age 21, as generally required under WIA).[37]

Timing of Funds

Section 189(g)(1)(A) of WIA requires that funds obligated for a program or activity carried out under Title I of the act are available for obligation only on the basis of a program year.[38] The program year begins on July 1 in the fiscal year for which the appropriation is made and ends June 30 of the following year. Under Section 189(g)(1)(B), funds for Youth Activities may first become available for a new program year in the preceding April. In addition, Congress has tended to specify that funds appropriated for YouthBuild and the youth component of the Reintegration of Ex-Offenders program are available for obligation beginning in the April preceding a given program year.[39]

Pursuant to Section 189(g)(2), funds obligated for any program year for a program or activity carried out under Title I may be expended by each state receiving such funds during that program year and the two succeeding program years.[40] Local areas may expend funds received from the state during the program year and the succeeding program year. Congress has generally required that obligated funds for Job Corps are made available for one program year, although funding for certain purposes can be obligated through later dates.

The next section of the report provides further discussion about the five youth programs authorized under Title I of WIA.

Youth Activities Formula Grant Program[41]

Overview and Purpose

The Youth Activities formula grant program is one of three state formula grant programs authorized by WIA. The other two programs target adults (Adult Activities) and dislocated workers (Dislocated Worker Activities), although youth ages 18 or older are eligible for services

---

[37] U.S. Congress, U.S. House of Representatives. *Making Supplemental Appropriations for Job Preservation and Creation, Infrastructure Investment, Energy Efficiency and Science, Assistance to the Unemployment, and State and Local Fiscal Year Ending September 30, 2009, and For Other Purposes*, 111th Cong., 1st sess., February 12, 2009, H.Rept. 1116-16.

[38] Section 173(h)(2), which pertains to authorization for YouthBuild, states that notwithstanding Section 189(g), appropriations for any fiscal year for programs and activities carried out under this section are to be available for obligation only on the basis of a fiscal year.

[39] For information about the timing of funding under the three WIA formula grant programs—Adult, Dislocated Workers, and Youth—see Congressional Distribution Memorandum, *Issues Related to Workforce Investment Act (WIA) Funding*, by David H. Bradley. Available upon request.

[40] Funds obligated for any program year for a pilot or demonstration program (Section 171) are to remain available until expended.

[41] Title I, Chapter 4 of the Workforce Investment Act and 20 C.F.R. 664.

provided through the Adult Activities program. These programs provide core funding for a coordinated system of employment and training services overseen by a state workforce investment board (WIB) and the governor, and comprised of representatives of businesses and other partners. The WIA Youth Activities formula grant program is arguably the centerpiece of the federal youth job training and employment system. As specified in the law, the program has several purposes: to provide assistance in achieving academic and employment success through activities that improve educational and skill competencies and foster effective connections to employers; to ensure ongoing adult mentoring opportunities for eligible youth; to provide opportunities for training, continued supportive services, and participation in activities related to leadership, citizenship, and community service; and to offer incentives for recognition and achievement to youth.

Unlike JTPA, which had two separate programs for summer and year-round activities, WIA funds both under the Youth formula program. WIA also mandates that certain elements be made available to all youth participants through Youth Activities, including summer opportunities linked to academic and occupational learning (see **Table 2**). Under JTPA, several of these elements were either optional or not present. In addition, the Youth program requires that 30% of WIA youth funds be spent on out-of-school youth. While JTPA's Youth Training Program required half of all youth to be out of school, the larger summer youth program did not set any requirements for this population.

Program Structure

DOL provides funding to state WIBs based on their relative[42] unemployment and youth poverty status.[43] In turn, the state WIBs distribute 85% of funds, also based on unemployment and poverty factors, to local workforce areas that are designated by the governor. The state retains as much as 15% for statewide activities.[44] A local area is overseen by the local WIB. Membership of the local WIB includes representatives of businesses, local education entities, labor organizations, community-based organizations, and economic development agencies, among others. Local WIBs, in coordination with their youth councils (discussed below), competitively award funds to local organizations and other entities to provide employment and job training services to youth. A 2004 report by the Government Accountability Office (GAO) examined the entities that local WIBs contract with to provide these services. Based on a survey of all local WIBs, the report found that about half of all youth received Youth Activities services through community-based organizations, secondary schools, and colleges or universities.[45] A smaller share of youth received

---

[42] The word "relative" as used in this report means the number of individuals in a state compared to the total number in all states.

[43] Under WIA, of the funds appropriated for Youth Activities, not more than 0.25% is reserved for outlying areas and not more than 1.5% is reserved for Youth Activities for Native Americans. The remainder of funds are allocated to states by a formula based one-third on the relative number of unemployed individuals residing in areas of substantial unemployment (an unemployment rate of at least 6.5%), one-third on the relative "excess" number of unemployed individuals (an unemployment rate more than 4.5%), and one-third on the relative number of low-income youth. Section 127(b) of WIA.

[44] Alternatively, a state may distribute to local areas a portion equal to not less than 70% of the funds they would have received using the employment and poverty factors, with the remaining portion of funds allocated on the basis of a formula that incorporates additional factors relating to excess youth poverty in urban, rural, and suburban local areas and excess unemployment above the state average in these areas. Such a formula must be developed by the state WIB and approved by the DOL Secretary as part of the state plan. Section 128(b)(3) of WIA.

[45] The report found that in-school youth were most likely to receive services through—in this order—community
(continued...)

services through one-stop centers (discussed below) and other entities, such as local or state governments and private employers.

With assistance from the state WIB, the governor develops a five-year plan that addresses several items related to employment and training needs, performance accountability, and employment and training activities. The plan must address items specific to Youth Activities (Section 112), including a description of the factors used to distribute funds to local areas for Youth Activities; the state's strategy for providing comprehensive services to eligible youth, particularly those who have significant barriers to employment; the criteria used by local boards in awarding and assessing providers for youth activities' grants; and a description of how the state will coordinate Youth Activities with services provided by Job Corps and Youth Opportunity grants, where applicable.

The local WIB develops a local plan that discusses items similar to those in the state plan, except that the plan describes the local area's one-stop delivery system, which is comprised of partners that collaborate to provide coordinated employment and training services in the community. Nearly 20 federal programs must provide services through the one-stop system, either by co-location, electronic linkages, or referrals. A local program funded by the Youth Activities formula grant program and the one-stop workforce system are encouraged to work together to facilitate the coordination and delivery of comprehensive, longer-term workforce services for youth.[46] In fact, as a required partner in the one-stop system, a local program must use a portion of its funds to create and maintain the one-stop delivery system and enter into a memorandum of understanding with the local WIB relating to the operation of the one-stop, among other requirements.[47]

Youth Councils

Each local WIB is required under law to establish a local youth council (Section 117(h)). Together, the WIB and the youth council oversee a local youth program funded by Youth Activities. The purpose of the youth council is to provide expertise in youth policy and to assist the local board in developing portions of the local plan relating to eligible youth. As specified in the law, the councils must coordinate youth activities in a local area, develop portions of the local plan related to eligible youth, recommend eligible providers of youth activities to be competitively awarded grants or contracts, oversee the activities of the providers, and carry out other duties specified by the local WIB.

(...continued)

organizations, secondary schools, colleges or universities, youth one-stop centers, adult one-stop centers, and other providers, such as local or state governments. Out-of-school youth were most likely to receive services through—in this order—community organizations, colleges or universities, secondary schools, adult one-stop centers, youth adult one-stop centers, and other providers, such as local or state governments. U.S. General Accounting Office, *Workforce Investment Act: Labor Actions Can Help States Improve Quality of Performance Outcome Data and Delivery of Youth Services*, GAO-04-308, February 2004, pp. 17-19. (GAO is now known as the Government Accountability Office.)

[46] U.S. Department of Labor, Employment and Training Administration, Training and Employment Guidance Letter (TEGL) No. 9-00 ("Workforce Investment Act of 1998, Section 129—Competitive and Non-competitive Procedures for Providing Youth Activities Under Title I"), January 31, 2001; and U.S. Department of Labor, Employment and Training Administration, TEGL No. 16-00 ("Availability of Funds to Support Planning Projects that Enhance Youth Connections and Access to the One-Stop System"), March 19, 2001. (Hereinafter, U.S. Department of Labor, Employment and Training Administration, TEGL No. 16-00, March 19, 2001.)

[47] U.S. Department of Labor, Employment and Training Administration, TEGL No. 16-00, March 19, 2001.

The youth council is comprised of members of the local board with special interest or expertise in youth policy; representatives of youth service, juvenile justice, and local law enforcement agencies; representatives of local public housing authorities; and parents of eligible youth seeking assistance through the adult activities or dislocated workers activities, among others. A 2002 study by GAO of the Youth Activities program included survey data about the membership of local youth councils. At the time, 92% of youth councils included participants from youth-serving agencies and 93% included people who had experience in youth activities. Seventy-five percent of youth councils had personnel from public housing authorities and 71% included parents of WIA-eligible youth. Most youth councils expanded their membership to include optional representatives, such as local educators.[48]

Elements of Local Programs

Local programs are responsible for carrying out the purposes of the act. In addition to assessing the skills of youth who receive services, local programs must provide 10 activities or "elements" to youth, as summarized in **Table 2**. DOL classifies elements based on whether they are targeted to educational achievement, summer employment, employment services, leadership development activities, or additional support for youth services. In addition, programs must provide follow-up services.[49] Note that although local WIBs must make all 10 program elements available to youth, each individual youth does not need to participate in all elements. Further, local programs that receive Youth Activities funding need not provide all 10 program elements if certain services are already accessible for all eligible youth in the area; however, these other services must be closely coordinated with the local programs.[50] Local WIBs must provide to each youth information on the fully array of applicable or appropriate services available through the local board, other eligible providers, or one-stop partners, and they must also refer youth to appropriate training and educational programs, among other activities.

Table 2. Elements of Youth Programs Funded by WIA Youth Activities Formula Grant Program

Educational achievement

- Tutoring, study skills training, and instruction leading to completion of secondary school, including dropout prevention strategies.

- Alternative secondary school services, as appropriate.

Summer employment opportunities

- Summer employment opportunities that are directly linked to academic and occupational learning.

Employment services

- As appropriate, paid and unpaid work experiences, including internships and job shadowing.

---

[48] U.S. General Accounting Office, *Workforce Investment Act: Youth Provisions Promote New Service Strategies, but Additional Guidance Would Enhance Program Development*, GAO-02-213, April 2002, pp. 20-21. (GAO is now known as the Government Accountability Office.)

[49] These elements are classified in the Workforce Investment Act Standardized Record Data (WIASRD) Data Book.

[50] Department of Labor, Employment and Training Administration, Training and Employment Guidance Letter (TEGL) No. 9-00, January 23, 2001; and Department of Labor, Employment and Training Administration, Training and Employment Guidance Letter (TEGL) No. 18-00, April 23, 2001. Local WIBs are advised to establish ongoing relationships with non-WIA funded activities that provide services for WIA-eligible youth.

- Occupational skill training, as appropriate.

Leadership development activities

- Leadership development opportunities, which may include, but are not limited to, community service and peer-centered activities encouraging responsibility and other positive social behaviors during non-school hours, as appropriate; community and service learning projects; organizational and teamwork training, including team leadership training; and citizenship training, including life skills training such as parenting, work behavior training, and budgeting of resources, among other activities.

Additional support for youth services

- Supportive services.

- Adult mentoring for the period of participation and a subsequent period, for a total of not less than 12 months.

- Comprehensive guidance and counseling, which may include drug and alcohol abuse counseling and referral, as appropriate.

Follow-up services

- Follow-up services for not less than 12 months after the completion of participation, as appropriate; follow-up services for youth include regular contact with a youth participant's employer, including assistance in addressing work-related problems that arise; assistance in securing better jobs, career development, and further education; work-related peer groups; adult mentoring; and tracking the progress of youth in employment after training.

Source: Congressional Research Service, based on Section 129(c)(2) of the Workforce Investment Act and Department of Labor, *WIASRD Data Book*, Appendix B.

What Elements Mean in Practice[51]

As part of a 2004 survey of local WIBs, GAO found that most local programs used multiple service providers to deliver youth services, although some used a small number. For example, a single WIA provider in rural Wisconsin delivered all 10 elements in a long-term, year-round program for out-of-school youth. Youth participants worked in teams to build or refurbish low-income housing. At the building sites, youth received paid employment, occupational training, leadership training, and mentoring from an adult supervisor. Off site, youth received classroom instruction to prepare for their high school equivalency exam; career counseling; and support services, such as meals and health care. Upon exiting, they received monthly follow-up services for at least two years.

According to the GAO report, schools were also used as youth service providers. Many of the schools provided youth services directly or collaborated with other education providers. For instance, an education provider in New Jersey collaborated with local school districts, universities, and private businesses to operate a program designed to help youth explore careers in the food industry. During the summer, 30 in-school youth ages 14 through 16 learned basic job skills in the classroom, visited farms and food businesses, and worked at local food businesses and restaurants. During the school year, students were placed in paid internships in the food industry and received mentoring services from employers.

The 2004 report also discusses that local areas developed partnerships with the business community to deliver services. Over one-third of local WIBs reported that businesses subsidized work experience for WIA youth. Examples of the types of services provided to youth through

---

[51] See also CRS Report R40830, *Vulnerable Youth: Federal Funding for Summer Job Training and Employment*, by Adrienne L. Fernandes-Alcantara.

these partnerships include work readiness training, in issues such as punctuality, teamwork, respect for others, and appropriate dress, that businesses assisted with; and financial management curricula provided by businesses.

Finally, a 2004 report for DOL by Social Policy Research Associates drew on data from site visits to a small number of states and local areas in 2000 and 2001 to understand how the elements are carried out.[52] For example, paid and unpaid work experience entailed work experience in conjunction with other services to increase a youth's education and occupational skills. For instance, in Du Page County, IL, the local WIB developed paid and unpaid work experiences in information technology occupations, such as web design and computer maintenance.

Participants

A youth is eligible for the Youth Activities formula grant program if he or she is age 14 through 21,[53] is a low-income individual, and has one or more of the following barriers:

- deficient in basic literacy skills;

- a school dropout;

- homeless, a runaway, or a foster child;

- pregnant or parenting;

- an offender; or

- requires additional assistance to complete an educational program or to secure and hold employment.[54]

At least 30% of all Youth Activities formula grant funds must be used for activities for out-of-school youth, *or* youth who have dropped out or received a high school diploma or its equivalent but are basic skills deficient, unemployed, or underemployed.[55]

Older and Out-of-School Youth

Youth ages 18 through 21 may enroll in the Youth Activities formula grant program or Adult Activities program, or may co-enroll in both programs. Less than 1% of youth tend to enroll in both programs.[56] Participation in the adult program is based on a "sequential service" strategy that

---

[52] Social Policy Research Associates, *The Workforce Investment Act After Five Years: Results from the National Evaluation of the Implementation of WIA*, prepared for the U.S. Department of Labor, June 2004, http://www.doleta.gov/reports/searcheta/occ/papers/SPR-WIA_Final_Report.pdf.

[53] ARRA effectively authorizes programs funded by Youth Activities via the law to temporarily extend the age of eligibility from 21 to 24.

[54] These terms are defined in **Appendix B**. Up to 5% of youth participants in a local area may be individuals who do not meet the income criteria, but have at least one barrier to employment, some of which are not identical to those listed above: (1) deficient in basic literacy skills; (2) a school dropout; (3) homeless or a runaway; (4) an offender; (5) one or more grade levels below the grade level appropriate to the individual's age; (6) pregnant or parenting; (7) possess one or more disabilities, including learning disabilities; or (8) face serious barriers to employment as identified by the local WIB (20 C.F.R. 664.220).

[55] Title I, Section 101(33) of the Workforce Investment Act.

[56] Ibid, Table II-14.

consists of three levels of services. Any individual may receive "core" services (e.g., job search assistance). To receive "intensive" services (e.g., individual career planning and counseling), an individual must have received core services and need intensive services to become employed or to obtain or retain employment that allows for self-sufficiency. To receive training services (e.g., occupational skills training), an individual must have received intensive services and need training services to become employed or obtain or retain employment that allows for self-sufficiency.

Allocations

Funding for the Youth Activities formula grant program is allocated from DOL to states, including Washington, DC, and territories. Under current law, not more than 0.25% is reserved for outlying areas[57] and not more than 1.5% is reserved for youth activities in the Native American programs (Section 166). The remainder of the funds are allocated to states by a formula based one-third on the relative number of unemployed individuals residing in areas of substantial unemployment (an unemployment rate of at least 6.5%), one-third on the relative "excess" number of unemployed individuals (an unemployment rate of at least 4.5%), and one-third on the relative number of low-income youth. In addition, states receive, at minimum, the higher of 90% of their relative share of the prior year's funding or 0.25% of the total allocation, or at maximum, 130% of their relative share of the prior year's funding.[58]

Of the funds allocated to states for the Youth Activities formula grant program (as well as for the Adult and Dislocated Worker programs), not more than 15% can be reserved for statewide activities (Section 128(a)). States may use some of this funding for certain purposes related to youth activities, such as disseminating a list of eligible providers of youth activities and providing additional assistance to local areas that have high concentrations of eligible youth, among other

> ### Migrant and Seasonal Farmworker Programs for Youth
>
> Migrant and Seasonal Farmworker programs are authorized under Section 167 of WIA. Of appropriations exceeding $1 billion for Youth Activities, 4% is to be allocated to youth activities for farmworkers. The law specifies that every two years, DOL must, on a competitive basis, make grants or enter into contracts to carry out workforce investment activities (including those for youth) and provide related assistance for eligible migrant and seasonal farmworkers. These activities may include employment; training; educational assistance; literacy assistance; an English language program; workers' safety training; housing; supportive services; dropout prevention activities; follow-up services for those placed in employment, self-employment, and related business enterprise development; and technical assistance to build capacity in management information technology.
>
> Funds were allocated in FY1999 through FY2003 for workforce investment activities targeted to youth from migrant and seasonal farmworker families. The projects provided a variety of educational, employment, and youth development activities to migrant youth.
>
> Migrant youth can qualify for education and other services as dependents under the Adult Migrant and Seasonal Farmworker program authorized under Section 167 of WIA. Youth ages 18 and older can also be served as adults under the program.
>
> **Source:** Congressional Research Service correspondence with the U.S. Department of Labor, Employment and Training Administration, September 2009.

---

[57] The outlying areas comprise the U. S. Virgin Islands, Guam, American Samoa, the Commonwealth of the Northern Mariana Islands, the Republic of the Marshall Islands, the Federated States of Micronesia, and the Republic of Palau.

[58] In years where appropriations exceed $1 billion, the minimum allotments are the higher of (1) 90% of a state's relative share of the previous year's funding, (2) the amount the state received in 1998, or (3) 0.3% of the first $1 billion plus 0.4% of the amount over $1 billion.

activities. Funds may not be used to develop or implement education curricula for school systems in the state.

The balance of funding is allocated to local areas on the same basis that Youth Activities' funds are allocated to states, to take into account the relative numbers of unemployed individuals and low-income youth in that area compared to other local areas of the state (Section 128(b)). Local WIBs may reserve no more than 10% of funds allotted under the Youth program (and Adult and Dislocated Worker programs) for administrative costs. The local WIBs are responsible for competitively awarding grants or contracts to youth providers, based on the recommendations of the youth council and the criteria listed in the state plan (Section 117(d)(2)(B) and Section 123).

When funds exceed $1 billion, DOL is to reserve a portion for Youth Opportunity grants, discussed in more detail below, and the Migrant and Seasonal Farmworkers program (see text box above) before allocating funds to states. In addition, if appropriations exceeded $1 billion for youth activities for FY1999, DOL was to make available such sums as necessary for the Role Model Academy Project. Funds have not been appropriated for the Youth Opportunity grants and Migrant and Seasonal Farmworkers program since FY2003, the last year that Congress appropriated more than $1 billion for Youth Activities. The Role Model Academy Project received $10 million in FY1999 to establish a training academy for youth on an old military base. However, the project operated for only one year due to problems with the grant and the project did not enroll youth.[59]

Performance

Section 136 of WIA sets forth state and local performance measures as part of the accountability system. The measures, or "core indicators," for youth ages 14-18 are different than the indicators for youth ages 19-21, as shown in **Table 3**. The measures for younger youth focus on skill attainment and educational attainment. The older youth outcomes focus on employment. For each of the core indicators, the states negotiate with DOL to establish a level of performance. That is, the "measures" are identified in WIA Section 136, but the "levels" are determined by negotiation between states and DOL.[60] Measures are reported as part of the Workforce Investment Act Standardized Record Data (WIASRD), which also collects demographic and other information about youth, adults, and dislocated workers who exit the program .

ETA implemented a "Common Measures" policy for several workforce programs and revised the reporting requirements for WIA Title I programs.[61] Specifically, ETA introduced three youth

---

[59] According to the U.S. Department of Labor, Employment and Training Administration, the grantee spent all of the grant funds except for $12,355. An audit by the Office of the Inspector General (OIG) resulted in $262,258 in disallowed costs. The grantee appealed the determination, and the Department of Labor and the grantee entered into a settlement agreement in which the grantee agreed to pay $90,000. This is based on Congressional Research Service correspondence with the Department of Labor, Employment and Training Administration in October 2009.

[60] In their state plans, states must identify the expected (adjusted) level of performance for each of the core indicators for the first three program years of the plan, which covers five program years. In order to "ensure an optimal return on the investment of Federal funds in workforce investment activities," the Secretary and the governor of each state shall "reach agreement on the levels of performance" for all youth and other indicators identified in Section 136(b)(2)(A). This agreed-upon level then becomes the "state adjusted level of performance" that is incorporated into the plan.

[61] U.S. Department of Labor, Employment and Training Administration, Training and Employment Guidance Letter (TEGL) No. 18-04 ("Announcing the Soon-to-be Proposed Revisions to Existing Performance Reporting Requirements... "), February 28, 2005.

measures, as listed in **Table 3**. It is important to note, however, that ETA specifically indicated that the Common Measures were not to supersede the existing statutory performance reporting requirements for WIA. Despite this, DOL has granted waivers to multiple states to permit implementation of and reporting on only the Common Measures rather than on the current, fuller array of measures in WIA for youth, adults, and dislocated workers.[62]

Table 3. Statutory and Common Measures for WIA Youth Programs

	WIA Statutory Measures	Common Measures
Youth (ages 14 through 18)	• *Skill Attainment Rate:* (Number of basic skills goals attained + Number of work readiness skills goals attained + Number of occupational skills goals attained)/ (Number of basic skills goals set + Number of work readiness skills goals set + Number of occupational skills goals set). • *Diploma or Equivalent Attainment Rate:* Number of younger youth attaining secondary school diploma or equivalent by end of 1st quarter after exit / Number of younger youth exiters during exit quarter. • *Retention Rate:* Number of youth in postsecondary education, advanced training, employment, or apprenticeships / Number of younger youth exiters during exit quarter.	• *Placement in Employment and Education:* Number of youth in employment (including the military) or enrolled in post-secondary education and/or advanced training or occupational skills training in the first quarter after the exit quarter / Number of youth exiters during the exit quarter. • *Attainment of a Degree or Certificate:* Number of youth participants who attain a diploma, GED, or certificate by the end of the third quarter after the exit quarter / Number of youth exiters during the exit quarter. • *Literacy or Numeracy Gains:* Number of youth participants who increase one or more educational functional levels / Number of youth participants who have completed a year in the program (i.e., one year from the date of first youth program service) + the number of youth participants who exit before completing a year in the program.
Youth (ages 19 through 21)	• *Entered Employment Rate:* Number of older youth employed in 1st quarter after exit quarter / Number of older youth exiters during the exit quarter. • *Employment Retention Rate at Six Months:* Number of older youth employed in 3rd quarter after exit / Number of older youth exiters during the exit quarter. • *Earnings Change in Six Months:* Earnings in 2nd and 3rd quarter after exit minus earnings in 2nd and 3rd quarter prior to participation / Number of older youth exiters during the exit quarter. • *Credential/Certificate Rate:* Number of older youth employed, in postsecondary education, or in advanced training after 1st quarter of exit and received credential by end of 3rd quarter / Number of older youth exiters during the exit quarter.	

---

[62] U.S. Department of Labor, Employment and Training Administration, "WIA Waiver Authority: Increased Flexibility and Improved Programmatic Outcomes, Summary of WIA Waivers," at http://www.doleta.gov/waivers/.

Source: Congressional Research Service, based on the Workforce Investment Act of 1998 (P.L. 105-220), ETA Training and Employment Guidance Letter (TEGL) No. 7-99 ("Core and Customer Satisfaction Performance Measures for the Workforce Investment System "), March 3, 2000, and ETA TEGL No. 17-05 ("WIA Title IB Performance Measures and Related Clarifications," Attachment D), February 17, 2006.

Note: Some of the terms, such as "basic skills goals," "credential," and "certificate" are defined in **Appendix B**.

The next section of the report discusses, in less detail, four additional programs for youth that are authorized under WIA.

Job Corps[63]

Overview and Purpose

The Job Corps program is carried out by the Office of Job Corps within the Office of the DOL Secretary,[64] and consists of residential centers throughout the country. The purpose of the program is to provide disadvantaged youth with the skills needed to obtain and hold a job, enter the Armed Forces, or enroll in advanced training or higher education. In addition to receiving academic and employment training, youth also engage in social and other services to promote their overall well-being.

Program Structure

Currently, 125 Job Corps centers operate throughout the country and two more are scheduled to open in the coming few years.[65] Of these 125 centers, 28 of the sites are known as Civilian Conservation Corps Centers, which are operated by the U.S. Forest Service, an agency within the Department of Agriculture.[66] Programs at these sites focus on conserving, developing, or managing public natural resources or public recreational areas. Most Job Corps centers are located on property that is owned or leased long-term by the federal government.

Job Corps centers may be operated by a federal, state, or local agency; an area vocational education school, or residential vocational school; or a private organization. Authorization and funding for new Job Corps centers are contained in appropriations law. DOL initiates a competitive process seeking applicants that are selected based on their ability to coordinate activities in the workforce system for youth, their ability to offer vocational training opportunities that reflect local employment opportunities, past performance, proposed costs, and other factors.

Job Corps campuses include dormitories, classrooms, workshops for various trades, wellness (or health) centers, a cafeteria, a career services building, and administrative buildings. Each Job

---

[63] Title I, Subtitle J of the Workforce Investment Act and 20 C.F.R. 670.

[64] Since FY2006, Congress has directed DOL to operate the Job Corps Office in the Office of the Secretary. Federal regulations established the Office of Job Corps within the Office of the Secretary, pursuant to Secretary's Order 09-2006. U.S. Department of Labor, "Establishment of the Office of Job Corps Within the Office of the Secretary; Delegation of Authority and Assignment of Responsibility to Its Director and Others," 71 *Federal Register* 16192, March 30, 2006.

[65] For the most recent number of centers, see the U.S. Department of Labor, *Budget Justifications of Appropriation Estimates for Committee on Appropriations*, http://www.dol.gov/dol/budget/.

[66] DOL transfers funding for these centers to USDA under an interagency agreement.

Corps center must develop standards for student conduct and implement a zero tolerance policy for violence and drug and alcohol use. Students are dismissed from the program if they violate this policy. Centers also follow detailed guidelines about all aspects of the program as they are outlined in the Policy and Requirements Handbook.[67]

Services

Students may participate in the Job Corps program for up to two years. While at a Job Corps center, students receive the following services:

- academic, vocational, employment, and social skills training;

- work-based learning, which includes vocational skills training and on-the-job training; and

- counseling and other residential support services, including transportation, child care, a cash clothing allowance or clothing that is needed for participating in the program, and living and other allowances.

Students tend to experience the program in four stages.[68] In the *first phase*, students learn about the program and center through orientation sessions and other outreach efforts conducted by the center and its contractor for outreach and admissions. Students who decide they want to pursue the program and are selected participate in the *second phase,* which emphasizes career preparation, in the first few weeks of the program. Students learn about life at the center and focus on personal responsibility, social skills, and career explanation. Students also receive assessments of their abilities in math and reading, and they work with staff to develop and commit to what is known as a Personal Career Development Plan (PCDP). This plan includes the students' personal, academic, and career goals, which are evaluated as they progress through the program.

The *third phase* focuses on career development and is the stage at which most youth spend the majority of their time in the program. During this period, students learn and demonstrate career technical, academic, and employability skills. Training focuses on academic subject matters and how they are applied to specific trades or occupations. Students who did not graduate from high school can pursue a high school diploma or GED. Most Job Corps centers have developed a high school diploma program for their students through partnerships with public, private, and/or charter schools. Students who have already graduated focus on developing their technical skills at the center and on work sites under the direction of Job Corps' employer partners. Job Corps centers offer several technical training clusters. The clusters that are most commonly offered are construction, business and finance, health care, hospitality, manufacturing, automotive and machine repair, information technology services, renewable resources and energy, retail, and transportation.[69] During this period, students also begin to look for a job and learn how to identify and access the support services that are needed to live independently.

---

[67] U.S. Department of Labor, Office of Job Corps, *Policy and Requirements Handbook,* http://www.jobcorps.gov/Libraries/pdf/prh.sflb.

[68] Ibid.

[69] U.S. Department of Labor, Office of Job Corps, *Job Corps Annual Report: Program Year July 1, 2006—June 30, 2007,* pp. 18-21, http://www.jobcorps.gov/Libraries/pdf/py06report.sflb.

Finally, in the *fourth phase,* students participate in a period of career transition, in which they receive placement services that focus on placing them in full-time jobs that are related to their vocational training and pay wages that allow them to be self-sufficient, or placing them in higher education or advanced training programs, including apprenticeship programs. For one year after exiting the program, graduates must receive services that include transition support and workplace counseling. Some graduates may go on to participate in advanced training. These students continue to remain in the program for another year while obtaining additional training and education, such as an Associate's Degree.

Job Corps centers provide services both on-site and off-site, and contract some of these services. Centers rely on outreach and admissions contractors to recruit students to the program. These contractors may include a one-stop center, community action organizations, private for-profit and nonprofit businesses, labor organizations, or other entities that have contact with youth. Contractors seek out potential applicants, conduct interviews with applicants to identify their needs and eligibility status, and identify youth who are interested and likely Job Corps participants. Similarly, centers rely on placement agencies—organizations that enter into a contract or other agreement with Job Corps—to provide placement services for graduates and, to the extent possible, former students. Services such as vocational training are sometimes provided by outside organizations, such as the Home Builders Institute.

In addition, each Job Corps center must have a business and community liaison designated by the center director to establish relationships with employers, applicable one-stop centers and local boards, and other stakeholders. Each center must also establish an Industry Advisory Council, comprised of employers; representatives of labor organizations, where present, and employees; and Job Corps students and graduates. A majority of the members must be local and distant business owners, chief executives or chief operating officers of non-governmental employers, or other private sector employers, and they must have substantial management and other responsibilities and represent businesses with employment opportunities for youth in the program. The council must work with local WIBs and review local market information to provide recommendations to the center director about the center's education and training offerings, including emerging occupations that would suitable for training.

Finally, each center must establish a Community Relations Council to serve as a liaison between the center and the surrounding communities.[70] The councils are to be comprised of representatives of business, civic, and educational organizations; elected officials; representatives from law enforcement agencies; other service providers; students; and staff. Centers must provide opportunities for students and staff to participate in community service activities on a regular basis.

Participants

Job Corps participants must be ages 16 through 24,[71] low-income, and facing one or more of the following barriers to education and employment: (1) basic skills deficient; (2) homeless, a runaway, or a foster child; (3) a parent; or (4) in need of additional education, vocational training, or intensive counseling and related assistance in order to participate in regular schoolwork or to

---

[70] Ibid.

[71] No more than 20% of participants may be ages 22 through 24 on the date of enrollment.

secure and maintain employment.[72] Notably, the program does not impose an upper age limit for students with disabilities. Job Corps centers take additional factors into consideration when selecting participants, such as whether the program can best meet their educational and vocational needs and whether the youth can engage successfully in group situations and settings. The applicant must also pass a background check that demonstrates he or she is not on probation or parole, or subject to similar findings. When selected for the program, students are usually placed at the site closest to their home. No more than 20% of participants may live off the grounds of the Job Corps center. Priority in non-residential placements is to be given to participants who are single parents.

Allocations

DOL enters into contracts with nonprofit and for-profit organizations, the Department of Agriculture, and the Department of Labor to operate the centers. Contracts are competitively awarded to organizations based on ranked scores, in conjunction with other factors. The contract period is two years, with three one-year-option renewals.

Performance

WIA specifies that Job Corps collect data on multiple measures related to performance and retention in the program. These measures pertain to graduation rates, graduates' entry into full-time or part-time unsubsidized employment, the average wage received by graduates at certain points in time, job retention at select points in time, entry into post-secondary education or advanced training programs, attainment of job readiness and employment skills, and the share of dropouts from the program, among other data. The program also collects information to assess performance through the Common Measures. As explained above, DOL introduced the Common Measures for WIA Title I programs in 2005. The Common Measures for Youth are placement in employment and education, attainment of a degree or certificate, and literacy and numeracy gains.[73] The measures in WIA and the Common Measures are interwoven into the Job Corps' performance management system that is used by the Job Corps Office to evaluate student performance and how well students are served at each of the centers.[74]

---

[72] Some of these terms are defined in **Appendix B**.

[73] See **Table 3** for a definition of these terms.

[74] The performance management system is comprised of four outcome measure systems: Outreach and Admissions (OA) Report Card, Center Report Card, Career Technical Training Reporting and Improvement System, and Career Transitions Services (CTS) Report Card.

YouthBuild[75]

Overview and Purpose[76]

In 2007, YouthBuild was transferred from the Department of Housing and Urban Development to DOL under the YouthBuild Transfer Act (P.L. 109-281). The program is authorized under WIA. As stated in the law, the purpose of YouthBuild is to (1) enable disadvantaged youth to obtain the education and employment skills necessary to achieve economic self-sufficiency in occupations in demand and post-secondary education and training opportunities; (2) provide disadvantaged youth with opportunities for meaningful work and service to communities; (3) foster the development of employment and leadership skills and commitment to community development among youth in low-income communities; and (4) expand the supply of permanent affordable housing for homeless individuals and low-income families by utilizing the energy of disadvantaged youth.

Program Structure

DOL competitively awards YouthBuild funds to organizations, which carry out the program in cooperation with subgrantees or contractors or through arrangements made with local education agencies and certain other entities. Entities that are eligible to apply for funding include a public or private nonprofit agency or organization, including a consortium of such agencies or organizations; community-based or faith-based organizations; entities that carry out activities authorized under certain other parts of WIA; community action agencies; state or local housing development agencies; an Indian tribe or agencies primarily serving Indians; state or local youth service or conservation corps; or any other entity eligible to provide education or employment training under a federal program.

While in the program, youth participate in a range of education and workforce investment activities, as listed in **Table 4**. These activities include instruction, skill building, alternative education, mentoring, and training in rehabilitation or construction of housing. Notably, any housing unit that is rehabilitated or reconstructed may be available only for rental by, or sale to, homeless individuals or low-income families; or for use as transitional or permanent housing to assist homeless individuals achieve independent living. In addition to construction activities, programs can support career pathway training targeted toward other high-demand occupations and industries offered within a YouthBuild program.[77] All educational programs, including programs that award academic credit, and activities supported with YouthBuild funds must be consistent with applicable state and local educational standards.

As specified in WIA, at least 40% of the time, youth must participate in certain work and skill development activities (these activities are denoted by footnote "a" in **Table 4.** At least an

---

[75] Title I, Subtitle D, Section 173A of the Workforce Investment Act.

[76] For an overview of the differences between the YouthBuild Program as administered by HUD and DOL, see U.S. Department of Labor, Employment and Training Administration, *YouthBuild Transfer Act: Synopsis and Section-by-Section Analysis*, http://www.doleta.gov/youth_services/YouthBuildSec-by-Sec%20Analysis%20FINAL.pdf.

[77] U.S. Department of Labor, "YouthBuild Program," 77 *Federal Register* 9122, February 15, 2012 (to be codified at 20 C.F.R. pt. 672).

additional 50% of the time, participants must be engaged in education and related services and activities designed to meet their educational needs (these activities are denoted by footnote "b" in **Table 4**.

Table 4. Eligible Activities Funded by YouthBuild, as Specified in the Workforce Investment Act (WIA)

Education and Workforce Investment Activities

Work experience and skills training, coordinated, to the maximum extent feasible, with pre-apprenticeship and registered apprenticeship programs, in the rehabilitation and construction activities described under "Supervision and Training," below. [a]

Occupational skills training.[a]

Other paid and unpaid work experiences, including internships and job shadowing. [a]

Services and activities designed to meet the educational needs of participants, including—(1) basic skills instruction and remedial education, (2) language instruction educational programs for individuals with limited English proficiency, (3) secondary education services and activities designed to lead to the attainment of a high school diploma or its equivalent; (4) counseling and assistance in obtaining postsecondary education and required financial aid, and (5) alternative secondary school services.[b]

Counseling services and related activities, such as comprehensive guidance and counseling on drug and alcohol abuse and referral.[b]

Activities designed to develop employment and leadership skills, including community service and peer-centered activities encouraging responsibility and other positive social behaviors, and activities related to youth policy committees that participate in decision-making related to the program.[b]

Supportive services and provision of need-based stipends to enable individuals to participate in the program, and supportive services to assist individuals, for a period not to exceed 12 months after the completion of training, in obtaining or retaining employment, or applying for and transitioning to postsecondary education. [b]

Job search assistance. [a]

Supervision and Training

Supervision and training for participants in the rehabilitation or construction of housing, including residential housing for homeless individuals or low-income families, or transitional housing for homeless individuals.

Supervision and training for participants in the rehabilitation or construction of community and other public facilities, except that not more than 10% of funds appropriated may be used for such supervision and training.

Other

Payment of administrative costs of the applicant, except that not more than 15% of the amount of assistance provided to the grant recipient may be used for such costs.

Adult mentoring.

Provision of wages, stipends, or benefits to participants in the program.

Ongoing training and technical assistance that are related to developing and carrying out the program.

Follow-up services.

Source: Section 173A of the Workforce Investment Act.

a. This activity counts toward the requirement that at least 40% of the time, youth must participate in certain work and skill development activities.

b. This activity counts toward the requirement that at least 50% of the time, youth must participate in education and related services and activities.

Participants

Youth are eligible for the program if they are (1) ages 16 through 24; (2) a member of a low-income family, a youth in foster care, a youth offender, an individual with a disability, a child of incarcerated parents, *or* a migrant youth; *and* (3) a school dropout.[78] However, up to 25% of youth in the program are not required to meet the income or dropout criteria, so long as they are basic skills deficient despite having earned a high school diploma, GED, or the equivalent; *or* have been referred by a high school for the purpose of obtaining a high school diploma.

Allocations

Grants are competitively awarded to organizations based on ranked scores, in conjunction with other factors, such as the applicant's potential for developing a successful YouthBuild program; the need for the program in the community; the applicant's commitment to providing skills training, leadership development, and education to participants; regional distribution of grantees; and the applicant's coordination of activities to be carried out with certain other stakeholders, including employers, one-stop partners, and national service and other systems; among other criteria.

DOL makes awards for three years (two years of program operations with a one-year period of follow-up). Applicants must provide cash or in-kind resources equivalent to at least 25% of the grant award amount as matching funds. Prior investments and federal resources do not count toward the match.

Performance

YouthBuild grantees report the Common Measures and two additional performance measures for all youth in the program. The two other measures are retention in employment or education and recidivism. Retention in employment and education tracks the share of young people who are employed or in an educational placement for each of the three quarters after exiting. The recidivism measure tracks the share of youth arrested and convicted of a new crime or parole violation within one year of enrollment.

Reintegration of Ex-Offenders[79]

Overview and Purpose

Section 171 of WIA authorizes DOL to conduct pilot and demonstration programs. The purpose of these programs is to develop and evaluate innovative approaches to providing employment and training services. In recent years, two programs have been specified in appropriations language and funded under the authority of Section 171. One of the programs—Reintegration of Ex-Offenders—is targeted, in part, to youth. A component of the program focuses on youth. (Other,

---

[78] Some of these terms are defined in **Appendix B**.

[79] Title I, Subtitle D, Section 171 of the Workforce Investment Act.

shorter-term programs that do not focus on youth offenders, per se, but do specifically target vulnerable youth have also been funded, as described in the text box below.) The youth component is comprised of related initiatives that seek to assist youth offenders and youth at risk of dropping out (or who have dropped out) with pre-release, mentoring, housing, case management, and employment services; to reduce violence within persistently dangerous schools through a combination of mentoring, educational, employment, case management, and violence prevention strategies; and to provide alternative education and related services for youth at risk of involvement with the justice system.[80]

Grants for youth offenders have been funded under WIA since FY2000.[81] The program was a stand-alone program until FY2008, when it was made a part of the Reintegration of Ex-Offenders program. It also supports the Prisoner Reentry Initiative (PRI) for adults. Funding for the program is authorized under both WIA and Section 112 (Responsible Reintegration of Offenders) of the Second Chance Act (P.L. 110-199), enacted on April 9, 2008. The Second Chance Act authorizes DOL to make grants to nonprofit organizations for the purpose of providing mentoring, job training and job placement services, and other comprehensive transitional services to assist eligible offenders ages 18 and older in obtaining and retaining employment.

Program Structure

The earliest initiatives for youth offenders, from FY1999 through FY2004, operated under what is known as the Youth Offender Demonstration Project (YODP).[82] The pilot funded 52 grantees to assist youth at risk of court or gang involvement, youth offenders, and gang members ages 14 to 24 in finding long-term employment. The more contemporary grant programs for youth offenders have funded multiple projects in recent years that have a focus similar to the earlier projects under YODP. Recent projects have included the School District Youth Offender Initiative; Persistently Dangerous Schools Initiative; Categorical Grants (Youth Offender Registered Apprenticeship, Alternative Education, and Project Expansion Grants); Beneficiary-Choice Demonstration; High Growth Youth Offender Initiative; Planning, State/Local Implementation, and Replication Grants; Civic Justice Grants; and Juvenile Offenders in High-Poverty, High-Crime Communities. Grantees include local and state governments, nonprofit organizations, including faith-based organizations; school districts; and community colleges.[83] These programs have been funded in at least one year since PY2006.[84] The projects are grouped below based on their focus. While the

---

[80] This is based on a review of initiatives funded by the Reintegration of Ex-Offenders program. U.S. Department of Labor, Employment and Training Administration, *Youth Services Discretionary Grants*, http://www.doleta.gov/Youth_services/Discretionary.cfm.

[81] This program was known as the Youth Offender Pilot Program, and funded 14 communities that provided educational, employment, re-entry, and other services to youth.

[82] The earliest funding for the program was authorized under Title IV of the Job Training Partnership Act. See U.S. Department of Labor, Employment and Training Administration, *Notice Inviting Proposals for Youth Offender Demonstration Projects*, August 28, 1998, http://www.doleta.gov/grants/sga/01-101sga.cfm.

[83] For a list of grantees and grant funding amounts, see U.S. Department of Labor, Employment and Training Administration, *Youth Services Discretionary Grants,* http://www.doleta.gov/grants/.

[84] Between PY2000 and PY2006, DOL used Youthful Offender funding to support the Serious and Violent Reentry Initiative at the Department of Justice; to award competitive grants to serve youthful offenders in 29 communities; to award non-competitive grants to several nonprofit organizations to serve young offenders and youth at risk of becoming offenders; and to award grants to eight states to improve the academic and workforce preparation programs in one juvenile correctional facility in each state.

projects each have a distinct purpose, their overall aim is to provide employment and other assistance to youth who are involved in the justice system, or are at risk of becoming involved.

Education

The School District Youth Offender Initiative, also known as the School District Gang Reduction grants, has focused on developing strategies for reducing youth involvement in gangs using a workforce development approach. The initiative is aimed at helping five public school districts—Baltimore; Chicago; Milwaukee; Orange County, FL; and Philadelphia—reduce the involvement of youth in gangs and violent crimes. Grant funds can be used for a range of education and employment interventions for youth who are involved, have been involved, or have a high risk of being involved in gangs or the juvenile justice system. Youth are eligible if they are in school and in grades 8-12, or are high school dropouts under the age of 21. School districts are required to partner with the local juvenile justice system, the mayor's office, the local WIB, the police department, and the U.S. Attorney's office in carrying out the program.

The Persistently Dangerous Schools Initiative has provided funding to three school districts—Berkshire Union Free School District in Canaan, NY; Baltimore; and Philadelphia—to improve outcomes of students in nine high schools that have been identified as persistently dangerous by the states' department of education, pursuant to the Elementary and Secondary Education Act. The grants fund a combination of new initiatives at each school, including reduced class size in core 9th and 11th grade English and math, which have a history of high rates of failure; a mentoring program using adult and peer mentors; career academies with particular themes; and a summer bridge program with remediation in English and math.

Apprenticeships, Alternative Education, and Expansion Grants

The Categorical Grants project has funded programs that provide apprenticeship opportunities and alternative education to youth who have been adjudicated (i.e., cases have been judicially determined) or are at risk of involvement in the justice system. The programs with apprenticeship opportunities prepare young adult offenders for in-demand careers in fields such as construction, welding, masonry, and advanced manufacturing. Programs with an alternative education focus are creating or enhancing schools to help young offenders earn diplomas and continue on to postsecondary education or jobs. Some grantees received funding to expand their programs to additional sites because of their records of successfully providing assistance to juvenile offenders. Grantees include state departments of corrections, schools boards, and nonprofit organizations.

Reentry[85]

Multiple grant programs focus on assisting young adults as they transition from the juvenile justice system. One of the programs is currently funded while others received funding in the recent past.

The Serving Juvenile Offenders in High-Poverty, High Crime Communities seeks to improve the long-term labor market prospects of juvenile offenders ages 16 to 24 in high-poverty, high-crime areas. The grants fund efforts at multiple sites to provide a combination of workforce development, education and training, case management, mentoring, restorative justice (to provide community service or other activities as a way to repair damage to the community), and activities to reduce community-wide violence. For example, the grant has funded the Latino Coalition for Faith & Community Leadership and Public/Private Ventures to support training opportunities for high school dropouts and young adult offenders ages 18 through 24 throughout the country.

The Beneficiary Choice Demonstration has provided funding to grantees to assist ex-offenders ages 18 through 29 transition from prison to the workplace. Participants may choose service providers from pools of faith-based and community groups. The grantees include the Arizona Women's Education and Employment, Inc., of Phoenix; the Colorado Department of Labor and Employment; the City of Chicago; the Indianapolis Private Industry Council, Inc.; and the Director's Council of Des Moines, IA. For example, Colorado's project focuses on delivering individualized, comprehensive offender reentry strategies through partners such as the Department of Corrections, Salvation Army, Grant Valley Catholic Outreach, one-stop centers, and Goodwill, among other entities. The project offers mentoring, counseling, housing, education, and training and employment opportunities in industries with high growth.[86] The project is working to increase its network to include all organizations that choose to provide offender services.

The High Growth Youth Offender Initiative has funded efforts to help former offenders gain the skills necessary to enter industries with high growth. Projects have focused on addressing the workforce needs of growing industries that provide employment opportunities and potential for advancement. Among the grantees are nonprofit organizations and workforce boards.

Finally, the Planning, State/Local Implementation and Replication Grants have funded four state juvenile justice agencies in the District of Columbia, Maryland, Texas, and Washington to serve

---

> ### Foster Care Youth Demonstration Project
>
> DOL awarded demonstration grants in 2005 and 2006 to five states—California, Illinois, Michigan, New York, and Texas—to design and implement programs to improve the self sufficiency, education attainment, and employment skills of youth aging out of foster care. The purpose of the grant, known as the Foster Care Youth Demonstration Project, was to encourage states to develop best practices around serving foster youth in the workforce investment system, and to integrate these practices across the state. The five states were required to target the programs to youth in areas with the largest foster care populations. DOL awarded each state $800,000 total; states were required to provide 100% matching funds. The programs served over 1,000 youth.
>
> **Source:** Congressional Research Service, based on Institute for Educational Leadership, Foster Care Youth Demonstration Project, *Final Evaluation Report, Executive Summary,* July 2008.

---

[85] Youth ages 18 and older may also be eligible to participate in the Prisoner Reentry Initiative (PRI), which seeks to reduce recidivism by helping former inmates find work when they return to their communities.

[86] For further information about DOL's recent efforts to fund initiatives that promote employment in high-growth industries, see CRS Report RL33811, *The President's Demand-Driven Workforce Development Initiatives*, by Ann Lordeman and Linda Levine.

all youth returning from juvenile correctional facilities to one county in the state; five counties to develop plans for serving all youth returning from correctional facilities to the local area; and YouthBuild Newark to develop YouthBuild programs serving juvenile offenders in four additional cities in New Jersey.

Community Service/Restorative Justice

The Civic Justice Corps Grants Serving Juvenile Offenders seeks to provide community service opportunities to juvenile offenders ages 18 to 24 who have been involved with the juvenile justice system within the past year. The purpose of the projects is to repair the harm they may have caused and to help rebuild relationships between the offender and members of the community. Programs funded under the grant are to provide the following: (1) meaningful community service projects and service learning opportunities; (2) educational interventions that lead to a credential and increase placement in post-secondary education and/or vocational training; (3) community connections that result in opportunities for offenders to rebuild trust; (4) high staff-to-participant ratios, including close adult supervision on community service projects; (5) career development components that seek to place each participant in a job, apprenticeship, or educational setting that leads to an industry-recognized credential; and (6) post-program support and follow-up.

> ### Multiple Education Pathways Blueprint
>
> The Multiple Education Pathways Blueprint is a one-time grant program funded under WIA's pilot and demonstration authority. In FY2007, DOL provided $3.4 million to seven midsize cities "to 'blueprint' and implement a system that can reconnect youth [who have dropped out of high school] to a variety of high quality, innovative multiple education pathways." Each city has built a partnership among multiple stakeholders to study the scope of the dropout problem, map the service and resources in their community, and assess efforts to reform high schools. Partners are currently planning or pilot testing new approaches to education, including identifying youth at risk of dropping out, launching new supports during the summer or first semester of high school, offering Saturday school programs that get youth back on track with their peers, and providing sector-based education and training programs.
>
> **Source:** U.S. Department of Labor, Employment and Training Administration, Multiple Education Pathways Initiative.

Participants

Each of the initiatives targets select groups of at-risk youth. However, the projects generally serve youth ages 14 and older (or 18 or older) who have been involved with or have a high risk of involvement in gangs or the juvenile justice system, or attend "persistently dangerous" schools, as reported by select states.

Allocations

Grants are competitively awarded to entities such as community-based organizations and state and local juvenile justice agencies, based on ranked scores and other factors, depending on the project. Notably, only schools that meet the criteria of "persistently dangerous," as specified by the states and as permitted under the Elementary and Secondary Education Act (ESEA), are eligible to apply for funds under the Persistently Dangerous Schools Initiative.[87] Allocations vary

---

[87] ESEA requires each state receiving funds under the act to establish and implement a statewide policy requiring that a student attending a persistently dangerous school, as determined by the state in consultation with a representative sample of local education agencies (LEAs), or a student who becomes a victim of a violent criminal offense on school grounds be allowed to attend a safe school within the LEA.

for each of the projects, but, generally, grantees have received grants of $1 million to $5 million for one or more years.

Performance

DOL has performance measures for each Youth Offender initiative. The standards vary for each initiative depending on the focus of the grants and the population of youth served. However, the program has uniform measures for the program overall: (1) percentage of youth ages 18 and older entering employment or enrolling in post-secondary education, the military, or advanced training/occupational skills training; (2) percentage of youth offenders ages 14 through 17 who recidivate; and (3) percentage of youth offenders ages 18 and older who recidivate.[88]

Youth Opportunity Grants

Overview and Purpose

The Youth Opportunity Grants program was funded from FY1999 through FY2003, and operated until 2005. As stated in WIA, the program was intended to provide employment, educational, and youth development activities to increase the long-term employment of youth who live in enterprise communities, empowerment zones, and high-poverty areas and who seek assistance. By definition, enterprise communities and empowerment zones are in low-income areas. The program enrolled 92,263 participants over the course of the grant period, of whom 52.7% were female; 51.9% were in school and 48.1% were out of school; and 58.9% were black, 22.4% Hispanic, and 11.2% American Indian or Native Alaskan. At enrollment, just over half of all participants were attending school (54.3%). This is compared to 68.3% of youth in the community overall who were attending school.

Program Structure

YOG funds were awarded to 36 communities, 24 in urban areas, 6 in rural areas, and 6 on tribal lands.[89] A local WIB was eligible to receive funding if it had been designated as an empowerment zone or enterprise community; was in a state without such a zone or community and was designated as a high-poverty area by the governor; or was one of two areas in a state designated by the governor as areas for which a local board could apply for the grant and that met certain poverty guidelines. Entities other than a local board were eligible to receive funding if they were a recipient under WIA's Native American programs (Section 136); served a community that met certain poverty guidelines; and were located on an Indian reservation or served Oklahoma Indians or Alaska Native villages or Native groups.

According to a December 2005 report by GAO about the YOG program, recipients of the funds included states, local WIBs, counties, cities, and other entities. These entities either provided

---

[88] U.S. Department of Labor, Employment and Training Administration, *Budget Justification of Appropriation Estimates for Committees on Appropriations, FY2012,* vol. I, p. TES-72.

[89] U.S. Government Accountability Office, *Youth Opportunity Grants: Lessons Can Be Learned from Program, but Labor Needs to Make Data Available,* GAO-06-53, December 2005.

---

services directly to youth, or entered into contracts with organizations. As required under WIA, grantees were required to provide a broad range of education, employment, and other related activities that are currently provided under WIA Youth Activities (see **Table 2**). In addition, grantees were required to implement youth development activities that addressed leadership development, citizenship and community service, and recreational activities.

The programs were carried out at centers in each community. YOG communities had as few as one or as many as 40 centers.[90] Centers included at least a couple of the following amenities: classrooms, recreational facilities, computer labs, career centers, health centers, and staff offices. Some centers operated out of local high schools. At least one of the programs established a charter school to provide alternative educational services to youth, while another had a recording studio for youth to record music. Program staff included case managers to help identify youth's needs and connect them to services and activities, as well as employment specialists to help youth look for, secure, and retain employment or help them transition to college. Program staff also followed up with youth. WIA required grantees to provide intensive placement services, as well as follow-up services for not less than two years after the youth completed the program.

A key feature of YOG was the networks that the grantees created in each community. According to the GAO report, the networks were often comprised of educational, occupational, and other providers for youth services. The networks were facilitated by formal arrangements among the partners and referrals to other organizations, such as those that provided GED preparation and clothing for interviews. Some participants at some of the centers had the opportunity to enroll part time at a community college to earn academic credit. Partners also provided referrals to the grantees.

Participants

Unlike other youth programs authorized under WIA, youth could participate in the YOG program as long as they lived in a community receiving funds. Therefore, youth did not have to show that they met income and other eligibility criteria.

Allocations

Funds were awarded to communities for a one-year period, with renewals in each of the four succeeding years. WIA required that grants were distributed equitably among local boards and other entities serving urban and rural areas, taking into account the poverty rate in these areas. Grant applicants were required to describe how the activities carried out at the YOG center(s) would be linked to the activities under the WIA Youth Activities program and the type of community support for the activities, among other requirements.

---

[90] Ibid.

Performance Measures

As specified under Section 167(f) of WIA, DOL set performance measures for the Youth Opportunity grants and negotiated with grantees on the levels expected to be achieved for each measure. The performance measures included a completion rate, placement rate, retention rate, participation rate, and enrollment rates for in-school and for out-of-school youth.

Appendix A. Workforce Investment Act Funding for Youth Programs

Table A-1. WIA Youth Activities State Allotments, PY2008-PY2011, Plus Funding Under the American Recovery and Reinvestment Act (ARRA, P.L. 111-5)

Includes allotments for outlying areas and Native Americans

State	PY2008 (P.L. 110-161)	ARRA (P.L. 111-5)	PY2009 (P.L. 111-8)	PY2010 (P.L. 110-351)	PY2011 (P.L. 112-5)	PY2012 (P.L. 112-74)
Total	$924,069,465	$1,188,000,000	$924,069,000	$924,069,000	$825,913,862	$824,353,022
Alabama	10,066,414	11,647,403	9,059,768	11,777,698	12,455,574	11,711,479
Alaska	3,401,753	3,936,018	3,061,576	2,755,418	2,216,462	2,024,817
Arizona	15,410,351	17,830,637	13,869,309	15,982,731	15,326,190	16,510,641
Arkansas	10,427,807	12,065,555	9,385,022	8,446,520	6,794,393	6,431,994
California	131,478,160	186,622,034	145,161,310	136,875,948	117,952,080	123,857,750
Colorado	10,263,091	11,874,970	9,236,777	11,132,070	9,788,025	11,882,561
Connecticut	7,422,406	11,034,723	8,583,204	8,869,254	8,060,872	8,794,724
Delaware	2,269,746	2,918,025	2,269,744	2,269,744	2,028,651	2,024,817
District of Columbia	3,430,967	3,969,821	3,087,869	2,779,082	2,402,872	2,323,591
Florida	25,652,600	42,873,265	33,348,363	43,352,872	50,372,277	53,892,125
Georgia	20,223,508	31,361,665	24,394,229	28,251,785	24,305,197	25,482,266
Hawaii	2,404,095	2,918,025	2,269,744	2,690,193	2,272,811	2,243,958
Idaho	2,290,478	2,918,025	2,269,744	2,950,667	3,428,419	4,027,145
Illinois	41,245,377	62,203,400	48,384,035	43,545,632	36,086,031	32,767,678
Indiana	20,463,638	23,677,573	18,417,265	19,697,136	16,043,006	15,457,182
Iowa	4,091,704	5,172,183	4,023,109	4,750,212	5,519,334	4,962,142
Kansas	6,155,030	7,121,714	5,539,524	5,930,458	5,248,975	5,511,824
Kentucky	14,567,756	17,709,821	13,775,333	14,303,105	12,514,937	12,676,374
Louisiana	17,295,855	20,012,271	15,566,262	14,009,636	11,269,372	11,409,318
Maine	3,280,785	4,293,710	3,339,802	3,476,520	2,887,584	2,831,274
Maryland	10,013,008	11,585,610	9,011,703	11,311,383	10,073,999	10,354,690
Massachusetts	21,466,585	24,838,038	19,319,917	17,387,925	15,988,686	15,009,154
Michigan	57,931,951	73,949,491	57,520,566	51,768,509	41,642,666	37,407,571
Minnesota	10,984,461	17,789,172	13,837,056	14,264,509	11,474,392	10,523,152
Mississippi	15,536,771	18,687,021	14,535,436	13,081,892	10,523,093	9,452,885
Missouri	19,654,610	25,400,077	19,757,091	17,781,382	14,549,044	15,108,428
Montana	2,269,746	2,918,025	2,269,744	2,344,418	2,174,750	2,405,630
Nebraska	2,544,921	2,944,616	2,290,428	2,518,508	2,288,141	2,207,155
Nevada	4,529,527	7,570,212	5,888,382	7,654,897	8,303,837	9,104,832

State	PY2008 (P.L. 110-161)	ARRA (P.L. 111-5)	PY2009 (P.L. 111-8)	PY2010 (P.L. 110-351)	PY2011 (P.L. 112-5)	PY2012 (P.L. 112-74)
New Hampshire	2,269,746	2,918,025	2,269,744	2,269,744	2,253,475	2,024,817
New Jersey	16,249,272	20,834,103	16,205,512	20,938,294	20,362,826	20,322,861
New Mexico	5,389,263	6,235,678	4,850,334	4,365,301	4,775,669	4,918,291
New York	54,654,801	71,526,360	55,635,768	51,835,670	46,253,787	45,892,839
North Carolina	19,061,803	25,070,698	19,500,888	25,351,154	24,598,968	23,736,834
North Dakota	2,269,746	2,918,025	2,269,744	2,269,744	2,028,651	2,024,817
Ohio	48,535,694	56,158,510	43,682,103	39,313,893	31,915,350	29,136,945
Oklahoma	7,526,029	8,708,036	6,773,423	6,970,582	6,877,913	6,676,111
Oregon	13,022,777	15,068,081	11,720,493	13,707,810	11,026,583	10,760,018
Pennsylvania	32,746,691	40,647,780	31,617,301	31,871,328	29,506,561	28,346,353
Puerto Rico	36,693,982	42,456,987	33,024,567	29,722,110	23,908,509	21,476,993
Rhode Island	3,357,319	5,611,097	4,364,513	4,531,698	3,767,218	3,687,520
South Carolina	21,357,908	24,712,293	19,222,108	17,299,897	13,916,063	12,754,206
South Dakota	2,269,746	2,918,025	2,269,744	2,269,744	2,028,651	2,024,817
Tennessee	19,653,705	25,099,116	19,522,993	18,716,506	16,288,215	15,784,120
Texas	70,870,137	82,000,708	63,783,091	57,404,782	52,833,195	55,664,646
Utah	4,379,351	5,067,154	3,941,414	3,547,273	4,121,624	5,347,985
Vermont	2,269,746	2,918,025	2,269,744	2,269,744	2,028,651	2,024,817
Virginia	9,462,211	12,982,612	10,098,341	13,127,843	13,540,444	13,020,339
Washington	20,263,008	23,445,432	18,236,698	17,997,280	15,992,583	16,959,549
West Virginia	4,618,029	5,343,318	4,156,224	3,924,261	4,315,932	4,577,244
Wisconsin	11,934,438	13,808,812	10,740,989	13,963,286	13,099,180	12,342,748
Wyoming	2,269,746	2,918,025	2,269,744	2,269,744	2,028,651	2,024,817
State Total	907,898,249	1,167,210,000	907,897,792	907,897,792	811,460,369	809,926,844
Outlying Areas Total	2,310,174	2,970,000	2,310,173	2,310,173	2,064,785	2,060,883
Native Americans	13,861,042	17,820,000	13,861,035	13,861,035	12,388,708	12,365,295

Source: Congressional Research Service presentation of U.S. Department of Labor, Employment and Training Administration, *State Statutory Formula Funding*, available at http://www.doleta.gov/budget/statfund.cfm.

Note: The program year for Youth Activities is July 1 through June 30, although funds may be made available on April 1, pursuant to Section 189(g)(1)(B) of the Workforce Investment Act. Funds for the program are available for two program years, including funds appropriated under ARRA. ARRA funds were available for two program years—PY2009 and PY2010, which extended through June 30, 2011. For purposes of the summer youth component, youth may participate in summer activities from May 1 through September 30, though it would appear that youth could participate only through the end of June in 2011.

a.   ARRA appropriated $1.2 billion for the Youth Activities program. Section 801 of ARRA permitted DOL to use 1% ($12 million) of funds for administration, management, and oversight of the program.

Appendix B. Definitions of Terms Used in WIA Youth Programs

- *Advanced training* refers to an occupational skills employment/training program, not funded under Title I of WIA, that does not duplicate training received under Title I. It includes only training outside of the one-stop, WIA, and partner system (i.e., training following exit). This measure is used as part of WIA statutory youth measures. (Training and Employment Guidance Letter 17-05, Attachment B, February 17, 2006.)

- *Advanced training/occupational skills training* refers to an organized program of study that provides specific vocational skills that lead to proficiency in performing actual tasks and technical functions required by certain occupational fields at entry, intermediate, or advanced levels. Such training should (1) be outcome-oriented and focused on a long-term goal as specified in the Individual Service Strategy, (2) be long-term in nature and commence upon program exit rather than being short-term training that is part of services received while enrolled in ETA-funded youth programs, and (3) result in attainment of a certificate (defined below). This measure is used as part of WIA youth common measures. (Training and Employment Guidance Letter 17-05, Attachment B, February 17, 2006.)

- *Basic skills goal* refers to a measurable increase in basic education skills, including reading comprehension, math computation, writing, speaking, listening, problem solving, reasoning, and the capacity to use those skills. This measure is used as part of WIA statutory youth measures. (Training and Employment Guidance Letter 17-05, Attachment B, February 17, 2006.)

- *Certificate* refers to a document awarded in recognition of an individual's attainment of measureable technical or occupational skills necessary to gain employment or advance within an occupation. These technical or occupational skills are based on standards developed or endorsed by employers. Certificates awarded by workforce investment boards are not included in this definition. Work readiness certificates are also not included in this definition. A certificate is awarded in recognition of an individual's attainment or technical or occupational skills by specified entities, such as a professional, industry, or employment organization, Job Corps Centers, etc. This measure is used as part of WIA youth Common Measures. (Training and Employment Guidance Letter 17-05, Attachment B, February 17, 2006.)

- *Credential* refers to a nationally recognized degree or certificate or state/locally recognized credential. Credentials include, but are not limited to, a high school diploma, GED, or other recognized equivalents, post-secondary degrees/certificates, recognized skill standards, and licensure or industry-recognized certificates. States should include all state education agency-recognized credentials. In addition, states should work with local workforce investment boards to recognize successful completion of the training services listed above that are designed to equip individuals to enter or re-enter employment, retain employment, or advance into better employment. This measure is used as part of WIA youth statutory measures. (Training and Employment Guidance Letter 17-05, Attachment B, February 17, 2006.)

- *Deficient in basic literacy skills* may be defined at the state or local level. The definition must include criteria to determine that an individual (1) computes or solves problems, reads, writes, or speaks English at or below the 8th grade level on a generally accepted standardized test or would receive a comparable score on a criterion-referenced test; or (2) is unable to compute or solve problems, read, write, or speak English at a level necessary to function on the job, in the individual's family, or in society. If the definition is established at the state level, the policy must be included in the state plan. (20 C.F.R. 664.205).

- *Ever in foster care* refers to a person who is in foster care or has been in the foster care system (as defined in WIASRD Data Book, Appendix B).

- *Individual with a disability* refers to an individual with any disability as defined in section 3 of the Americans with Disabilities Act of 1990. The act defines "disability" with respect to an individual as (1) a physical or mental impairment that substantially limits one or more major life activities of such individual; (2) having a record of such an impairment; or (3) being regarded as having such an impairment. "Being regarded as having such an impairment" refers to whether the individual establishes that he or she has been subjected to an action prohibited under the Americans with Disabilities Act because of an actual or perceived physical or mental impairment, whether or not the impairment limits or is perceived to limit a major life activity.

Low-income individual means an individual who:

(1) receives, or is a member of a family that receives, cash payments through a federal, state, or local income-based public assistance program;
(2) received an income, or is a member of a family that received a total family income (excluding unemployment compensation and certain other payments), for the six-month period prior to applying for youth employment and training activities, that, in relation to family size, did not exceed the higher of the poverty line, for an equivalent period, or 70% of the lower living standard income level, for an equivalent period;
(3) is a member of a household that receives food stamps[91] (or has been determined to be eligible for food stamps within the six-month period prior to applying for youth employment and training activities);
(4) qualifies as a homeless individual, as defined by the McKinney-Vento Homeless Assistance Act; or
(5) is a foster child on behalf of whom state or local government payments are made.

In cases permitted by DOL in regulations, an individual with a disability, whose own income meets the standards specified in the first two criteria but who is a member of a family whose income does not meet such requirements, may qualify (WIA Section (101)(25)).

---

[91] The Food Stamp program was recently renamed the Supplemental Nutrition Assistance Program (SNAP).

- *Occupational skills goal* refers to a measurable increase in primary occupational skills encompassing the proficiency to perform actual tasks and technical functions required by certain occupational fields at entry, intermediate, or advanced levels. Secondary occupational skills entail familiarity with and use of set-up procedures, safety measures, work-related terminology, record keeping and paperwork formats, tools, equipment and materials, and breakdown and clean-up routines. This measure is used as part of WIA statutory youth measures. (Training and Employment Guidance Letter 17-05, Attachment B, February 17, 2006.)

- *Out-of-school youth* means a youth eligible for services under Youth Activities who is a school dropout; or an eligible youth who has received a secondary school diploma or its equivalent but is basic skills deficient, unemployed, or underemployed (WIA Section (101)(33) and 20 C.F.R. 664.300).

- *Offender* means any adult or juvenile who (1) is or has been subject to any stage of the criminal justice process, for whom services under this act may be beneficial; or (2) requires assistance in overcoming artificial barriers to employment resulting from a record of arrest or conviction (WIA Section (101)(27)).

- *Pregnant or parenting youth* is an individual who is under 22 years of age and pregnant, or a youth (male or female) who is providing custodial care for one or more dependents under age 18 (as defined in WIASRD Data Book, Appendix B).

- *Requires additional assistance* refers to an individual who needs help in completing an educational program or securing and holding employment. The term may be defined at the state or local level. If the definition is established at the state level, the policy must be included in the state plan (20 C.F.R. 664.210).

- *School dropout* refers to an individual who is no longer attending any school and has not received a high school diploma or its equivalent. A youth's dropout status is determined at the time he or she registers for youth activities. An individual who is not in school at the time of registration and is subsequently placed in an alternative school may be considered an *out-of-school youth.*

- *Supportive services* means services such as transportation, child care, dependent care, housing, and needs-related payments that are necessary to enable an individual to participate in services provided by the Youth Activities program and other programs authorized under Title I of WIA. In addition, supportive services for youth also includes linkages to community services, referrals to medical services, and assistance with uniforms or other appropriate work attire and work-related tools, including such items as eyeglasses and protective eye gear (Section 101(46) of WIA, and as defined in WIASRD Data Book, Appendix B).

- *Work readiness skills goal* refers to a measurable increase in work readiness skills, including world-of-work awareness, labor market knowledge, occupational information, values clarification and personal understanding, career planning and decision making, and job search techniques (resumes, interviews, applications, and follow-up letters). They also encompass survival/daily living skills such as using the phone, telling time, shopping, renting an apartment, opening a bank account, and using public transportation; and include positive work habits, attitudes, and behaviors such as punctuality, regular attendance, presenting a neat appearance, getting along and working well with others, exhibiting good conduct, following instructions and completing tasks, accepting criticism from supervisors and co-workers, showing initiative and reliability, and assuming the responsibilities involved in maintaining a job. This category also entails developing motivation and adaptability, obtaining effective coping and problem-solving skills, and acquiring an improved self image. This measure is used as part of WIA statutory youth measures. (Training and Employment Guidance Letter 17-05, Attachment B, February 17, 2006.)

Author Contact Information

Adrienne L. Fernandes-Alcantara
Specialist in Social Policy
afernandes@crs.loc.gov, 7-9005

www.ingramcontent.com/pod-product-compliance
Lightning Source LLC
Chambersburg PA
CBHW081359170526
45166CB00010B/3138